Literature Reviews in Social Work

Literature Reviews in Social Work

Robin Kiteley and Chris Stogdon

Los Angeles | London | New Delhi
Singapore | Washington DC

Los Angeles | London | New Delhi
Singapore | Washington DC

SAGE Publications Ltd
1 Oliver's Yard
55 City Road
London EC1Y 1SP

SAGE Publications Inc.
2455 Teller Road
Thousand Oaks, California 91320

SAGE Publications India Pvt Ltd
B 1/I 1 Mohan Cooperative Industrial Area
Mathura Road
New Delhi 110 044

SAGE Publications Asia-Pacific Pte Ltd
3 Church Street
#10-04 Samsung Hub
Singapore 049483

© Robin Kiteley and Chris Stogdon 2014

First published 2014

Editor: Kate Wharton
Assistant editor: Emma Milman
Production editor: Katie Forsythe
Proofreader: Sharon Cawood
Indexer: Elizabeth Ball
Marketing manager: Tamara Navaratnam
Cover design: Shaun Mercier
Typeset by: C&M Digitals (P) Ltd, Chennai, India
Printed and bound by CPI Group (UK) Ltd, Croydon, CR0 4YY

Library of Congress Control Number: 2013937716

British Library Cataloguing in Publication data

A catalogue record for this book is available from the British Library

ISBN 978-14462-0126-8
ISBN 978-1-4462-0127-5 (pbk)

Robin: For my smart and smiley nephews, Owen and Ryan
Chris: For Kathleen and Ged – a mother and a brother loved like no other

Contents

About the Authors

Robin Kiteley is a Senior Lecturer in the Department of Behavioural and Social Sciences at the University of Huddersfield. He has taught academic study skills, information technology and research skills across a diverse range of subject areas including social work, criminology, politics, sociology and police studies. He has previously co-authored *Study Skills for Social Workers* for Sage.

Chris Stogdon is a social worker with extensive practice experience in both mental health and children's services. She has taught on social work courses for many years and been active in promoting representation of service users and carers in social work education. Her work includes practice education and the professional regulation of social work education. Currently she is working with Mothers Apart from their Children through Womenspace to include their voices in the social work curriculum. She has previously co-authored *Study Skills for Social Workers* for Sage.

Acknowledgements

Robin: Big snaps for Christian McGrath for being such a wonderfully generous and supportive friend, for keeping me going and for providing a much needed sanctuary. A massive thank you to my parents, Glen and Phil Kiteley, for basically supporting me every step of the way in life! It means the world to me. A huge thanks and bear hug for Ben Raikes, whose friendship, understanding and marvellous way with metaphors have brightened up many a day. Thanks to Gregory and Harrison for laughs, giggles and wicked dance moves. Finally, a heartfelt thanks to the colleagues who have supported me in this project, especially Kate McGuinn, and to the students I work with who have contributed to my thinking in so many ways.

Chris: I would like to thank all the people who have supported me in writing this work, including family, friends and colleagues from The University of Huddersfield, and special thanks to Guy, David and Anna for their love and patience.

Robin and Chris: We would both like to say a massive thank you to Emma Milman at Sage for her unflagging positivity, advice, feedback and patience. Thanks also to Alice Oven, Kate Wharton and Laura Walmsley for their support and advice along the way. A big thank you to Katie Forsythe for getting us through the production process. Finally, we'd like to thank our anonymous peer-reviewers, who provided some very helpful ideas and suggestions for the development of the manuscript.

Publisher's Acknowledgements

The Publisher would like to thank JISCMail and the Social Work-Alcohol-Drugs list administrator/owner for permission to use the screenshots in Chapter 4. They would also like to thank the Social Care Institute for Excellence (SCIE), ProQuest and Emerald for kindly granting permission to publish their material.

The screenshots in figures 4.2, 4.3, 4.4 and 4.5 are published with permission of ProQuest LLC. Further reproduction is prohibited without permission. Inquiries maybe made to: ProQuest LLC, 789 E. Eisenhower Pkwy, P.O. Box 1346, Ann Arbor, MI 48106-1346 USA. Telephone (734)761-4700; Email: info@proquest.com; Web-page: www.proquest.com

Introduction

☑ **Learning Outcomes** ☑

- To appreciate the relevancy of literature review processes for social work students and practitioners
- To gain an overview of the main features included throughout this book

Why Bother about Literature Reviews?

This book has been written to help social work students and professionals produce focused, well-researched and appropriately written literature reviews. There are several contexts in which you may be required to produce a literature review, including:

- Social work undergraduate or postgraduate programmes may require students to produce a project or dissertation, which is based around (or incorporates) a literature review.
- Research into social work practice is becoming increasingly 'evidence-based', which requires that practitioners and researchers are familiar with the findings that have been published in the literature around social work theory and practice.

The following chapters focus on (i) the practical steps involved in preparing and producing a literature review and (ii) the wider context in which literature reviews are used in social work learning and practice.

Features of this Book

We have incorporated various features into this book which are designed to:

- help you find relevant information
- provide you with opportunities to develop your skills
- prompt you to consider issues in more detail
- help you consolidate your learning and understanding
- extend your understanding through suggestions for follow-up activities.

Below is a brief summary of specific features.

Learning Outcomes

Each chapter begins with a bullet-pointed list of specific learning outcomes. Use these to get a quick overview of the key things you will be learning about.

Chapter Summaries

At the end of each chapter we have provided bullet-point summaries of the key points that have been addressed. This is intended to help with your recall of the main things that you have been reading about and, along with the 'Learning Outcomes' mentioned above, help you to navigate to relevant sections of the book.

Activities

While guidance and recommendations can help to put you on the right track, there is no substitute for trying things out for yourself. This is why each chapter contains a number of activities which are designed to get you actively involved in the processes that we describe.

It's useful to complete as many of these activities as possible, as they will help you to focus on your own learning, assess your own progress and also learn from any things that you get 'wrong'. Remember that some of the most valuable learning that we do can come from the things we struggle with or feel that we are getting wrong.

Many of the activities that we have devised feature extracts from real journal articles and other research sources. This is aimed to help you to become comfortable and familiar with the kind of material that you will need to read for your own literature review work.

Now take a few minutes to complete the introductory activity below.

ACTIVITY

Starting points...

This exercise is designed to help you to reflect on your current understanding of literature reviews, and what might be involved in the process of carrying out a literature review. Try to answer each question as fully as possible:

1. What does the phrase 'literature review' mean to you? You could answer this by thinking how you would define it, and also how you think you might go about doing it.
2. What is the value of a literature review in social work study or practice? What could social workers and students gain from undertaking a literature review?
3. List the different stages that you think are involved in carrying out a literature review.
4. What do you imagine will be the biggest challenge (for you personally) in carrying out your own literature review?

Did you know?

The 'Did you know?' boxes are designed to flag up quick snippets of information, such as definitions of key terms, explanations of key ideas or quick overviews of the context relating to particular issues. The following example illustrates this:

? Did you know? Referencing different types of information ?

A key requirement for effective literature reviews is that all sources used must be clearly and accurately cited and referenced. The format of a reference will vary depending on the type of publication that you are referencing. For instance, you may be familiar with the format of book, journal article and web page references, but did you know there is also a particular format for referencing:

- Electronic books
- Government/official documents
- Acts of Parliament
- ...and many other types of publication!

Chapter 9 looks at how to cite and reference your sources correctly, and also gives examples of the different types of reference that you are likely to need.

Think about...

The 'Think about...' boxes included in each chapter are designed to encourage you to stop and consider significant issues in relation to the literature review process, or in relation to your own learning process.

Think about... What counts as 'good' research?

A significant part of carrying out an effective literature review is not only being able to find relevant research literature on your chosen topic, but being able to provide a critical commentary on the quality of that research.

- What criteria (or 'yardsticks') would you put forward to help to assess the quality of the research literature that you will be reading?

We will look at assessing the quality of information sources in Chapter 4, and suggest ways of developing your critical and analytical skills in Chapter 6.

Case Studies

In some chapters case studies have been included to provide clear examples of how ideas, processes, methods or models have been used in practice. Focusing on particular cases can help us to grasp how general principles or abstract concepts can translate to the often messy and complex arena of 'real' life. This in turn can help us to develop more sophisticated and nuanced understandings of the academic resources that we use, along with their relative strengths and limitations.

Further Reading and Useful Resources

At the end of each chapter you will find some suggestions for further reading and resources which relate to the topic of that chapter. All of these suggested texts or resources are easily accessible, and some may be available through your institutional or local library service. Additionally, some chapters contain 'ideas for taking things further', which are follow-up activities that help to extend your knowledge and understanding of the topics addressed.

Getting Started

If you are entirely new to the process of carrying out a literature review, we would suggest that it would be helpful to work through this book in chapter order. The reason for this is that we have structured the book to reflect the order in which particular skills are used during the literature review process. Begin with Chapter 1, which will explain what a literature review is, and what a typical one might look like in terms of structure and contents.

If you are familiar with the literature review process, you may prefer to simply dive into the most relevant chapters for you, or the stage of the process that you are currently working on.

Chapter Summary

- We have briefly outlined why a book on literature reviews is relevant to social work students and practitioners.
- We have provided a quick overview of the main features of this book and have illustrated these with some examples.
- We have made some suggestions about where to begin with this book.

1

What is a Literature Review?

☑ **Learning Outcomes** ☑

- To understand what we mean by 'the literature' and evidence in social work
- To gain an awareness of what grey literature is, and why it is important
- To develop an awareness of the differing functions of literature reviews
- To gain an overview of narrative and systematic literature reviews
- To learn about the different methodologies employed in the literature review process

---

'The Literature' and Social Work Practice

What do we mean by 'the literature'?

'The literature' is the body of academic research that has been published and disseminated through publications such as books, academic journals, practitioner journals, websites and other sources. It's basically a shorthand way of referring to the sum of published knowledge about a particular subject. However, as you'll discover in more detail in Chapter 4, the idea of there being a coherent body of literature around a particular subject such as social work is becoming more problematic, as more and more publications appear in a variety of formats and contexts.

The nature of knowledge and evidence in social care practice

When discussing 'knowledge' in relation to social work, it can be easy to overlook some of the trickier questions about how we establish, define and verify what comes to be understood as knowledge. We might ask whether it is even possible to achieve consensus about what constitutes useful knowledge (particularly in respect of the way social workers carry out their practice). In the current socio-political context, social workers are increasingly under pressure to be able to justify their decisions and account for their actions, yet at the same time it would appear that ideas about what constitutes effective social work practice are frequently contested, and often not well-documented in terms of available research evidence.

Pawson et al. (2003) carried out a substantial investigation into the issue of types of knowledge in social care. They propose that the questions that should be asked of any piece of knowledge can be encapsulated in the useful acronym 'TAPUPAS':

Transparency   Is it open to scrutiny?
Accuracy   Is it well grounded?
Purposivity   Is it fit for purpose?
Utility   Is it fit for use?
Propriety   Is it legal and ethical?
Accessibility Is it intelligible?
Specificity   Does it meet source-specific standards?

ACTIVITY

Types and quality of knowledge in social care

For a flavour of some of the complex issues involved in considering the status and role of knowledge in social care practice, read the short 'Summary' section of Pawson et al.'s (2003) report, 'Types and quality of knowledge in social care', which is available at the following website address: www.scie.org.uk/publications/knowledgereviews/kr03.pdf

The use(s) of evidence

Increasingly, there is a demand for research in social work to establish evidence-based findings which can lead to replicable results in different settings. This ethos of evidence-based research comes from the domain of medicine and health care, and has gradually become more widespread in disciplines such as social care and education. Although there is recognition of the need for greater understanding of what is both effective and ineffective in social work practice, there is some disagreement as to whether evidence-based research can fulfil this role.

It should therefore be acknowledged that there are particular debates within the social work profession about the usefulness and appropriateness of evidence-based practice, with some claiming that it represents the best way of establishing better knowledge for practice, and others suggesting that it can minimise and overlook the importance of practitioners' localised knowledge. This has lead some commentators to point to 'evidence-informed' approaches (Hodson and Cooke, 2004: 12), which acknowledge the importance of empirical data, but which also recognise the importance of other sources of knowledge, such as practitioner knowledge, user and carer knowledge, organisational knowledge, research knowledge and policy community knowledge (Pawson et al., 2003). We will return to these, and other important issues relating to evidence-based practice, in more detail in Chapter 10.

Using the grey matter!

?   Did you know? What is grey literature?   ?

'Grey literature' has recently been defined as the various types of document produced by governments, academic institutions, businesses and industries

> that are protected by intellectual property rights, of sufficient quality to be collected and preserved by library holdings or institutional repositories, but not controlled by commercial publishers i.e., where publishing is not the primary activity of the producing body. (Schöpfel, 2010)

Basically, the term describes documents that may not have been published through conventional routes, and which may therefore be trickier to find and access. They can be thought to occupy a 'grey area' in comparison to traditional published material.

Examples of grey literature

Grey literature includes publications such as:

- newsletters
- policy documents
- some research reports
- minutes of meetings
- professional and regulatory body requirements
- leaflets
- internally printed reports
- unpublished undergraduate and postgraduate theses and dissertations
- unpublished conference papers
- blogs, tweets, bulletin board and other social media postings.

Why is grey literature useful or important?

Hartman (2006: 2) explains:

> Grey literature is particularly important in policy areas, where there are many issuing agencies such as think tanks, university-based research institutes, professional and trade organizations, advocacy groups, etc., all attempting to inform and influence the policy-making process.

Grey literature can promote a greater level of democracy and plurality in terms of the range of voices and opinions that are heard. However, it can also introduce some questions around issues of 'quality control', and it's important to be aware of both its strengths and limitations.

Grey literature – pros and cons

Table 1.1   Pros and cons of using grey literature

Pros	Cons
May cover issues which are very current and which have not yet been covered in the academic literature	Often not peer-reviewed and/or may not be checked by an editor – inaccuracies, inconsistency and errors may creep in
As it does not go through standard publishing processes, it can be made available very quickly and at a low cost	Reliability and validity are not guaranteed
Can provide important context to an issue or topic, particularly in relation to issues at the cutting-edge of social work practice	Often not indexed or catalogued – this can make finding it difficult
Can be more effective in terms of outlining local practice contexts which may have not come through as clearly in other literature	Some are in hard-copy format only – grey literature may have been printed in low print runs and may be difficult to access
	Online links to grey literature may only exist for a short time

?   Did you know? 'Reliability' and 'validity'   ?

These words are often used in the context of assessing the strengths and weaknesses of research processes, and you are likely to come across some discussion of them (and related issues) when reading about research methodology.
   In very broad terms:

- Reliability refers to the extent to which methods or findings are likely to yield similar results if the study, research, experiment or investigation were to be repeated in similar circumstances, using similar methods of investigation.
- Validity refers to the extent to which the research methods and instruments measure what they claim or set out to measure. An assessment of validity would also involve consideration of whether the results of a research process have been skewed or contaminated by additional (and sometimes unforeseen or unanticipated) factors in the research field and/or process.

Going grey

Time suggested: 20–30 minutes

Access the 'Review of grey literature on drug prevention among young people – Review Summary' at www.nice.org.uk/niceMedia/pdf/grey_lit_summary_v3FINAL.pdf (If the web link above is no longer active, use a search engine to find a current link to this document.)

Read the document (it is only five pages long so is quite quick to get through), and then answer the following questions:

1. What did this piece of work aim to do?
2. Why did they focus on grey literature?
3. How did they go about finding the grey literature?
4. Why was it important that the researchers applied critical appraisal criteria to the grey literature that they considered?
5. The 'Concluding remarks' section identifies several limitations of the grey literature that was reviewed. Can you identify three of these?

Introducing Literature Reviews

What is a literature review?

A literature review is a comprehensive summary of the ideas, issues, approaches and research findings that have been published on a particular subject area or topic. However, it is not a simple description of all that the reviewer has read on the topic. It is better understood as a critical synthesis (or bringing together) of:

- what can reasonably be asserted based on the extent of the literature findings
- what worked and didn't work in terms of methods of (and approaches to) investigation
- what can be gleaned from the range of theoretical perspectives that have been applied
- what gaps, inconsistencies or problems still need to be addressed in further research on the topic
- what results may reasonably be expected to be repeatable, and under what circumstances.

A good literature review will aim to 'weigh up the contribution that particular ideas, positions or approaches have made to the topic' (Hart, 1998: 9). Hart's quote emphasises the important critical and evaluative function of literature reviews. When you are preparing your own literature reviews, you will need to think about critically evaluating the research that you read. Of course, being 'critical' doesn't have to mean being 'negative' – you can also 'critically' examine the strengths and positive aspects of a piece of research.

What is the function and purpose of a literature review?

As a student or practitioner of social work you are most likely to encounter literature reviews in two main contexts:

1. Literature reviews as preparation for empirical research

A literature review is normally carried out prior to the design and implementation of the primary research methods in the case of empirical research studies. They may also be required for proposals for funding applications for research projects. In this context, the primary purposes of the literature review are:

- **To establish what has already been investigated** – therefore, researchers are far less likely to 're-invent the wheel' by simply repeating things which have already been done before.
- **To establish what methods and methodologies have already been used in the topic area** – this guides the researcher(s) in considering the most appropriate methods for their research investigation and highlights the affordances and limitations of particular methodological perspectives.
- **To establish what worked in terms of the research process** – the literature should flag up both the strengths and limitations of previous research tools/approaches and alert the researcher to potential challenges that may be associated with such resources.
- **To identify and build on the gaps in knowledge** – conducting a literature review should provide a degree of confirmation that what the researcher is planning to do is original, innovative and/or useful in some way.

2. Literature reviews as stand-alone pieces of work

Literature reviews can be carried out as a research methodology in their own right. In this case, the point of the literature review is not to prepare the way for empirical research, but instead to bring together what is known about a particular topic or issue in a way that hasn't previously been reported. The function of the literature review may therefore be to:

- consolidate understanding
- bring together findings from multiple sources
- map out the terrain of evidence in relation to a given issue
- highlight what is most convincing in the literature that has been published to date.

This in turn can serve a number of purposes, including:

- policy and practice development based on research evidence
- future research planning and development
- comparative understandings.

Is 'literature reviewing' a form of research?

There is some debate as to whether conducting a literature review, which is essentially concerned with secondary literature, can be considered to be a research process in its own right. Some commentators tend to view research as requiring the use of primary research methods, such as interviewing participants, devising and running questionnaires, carrying out observations of practice, and so on. If you are currently enrolled on an academic course at a university, you may find that a clear distinction is made between 'conducting research' and 'carrying out a literature review'. However, in reality the distinction is less clear-cut, particularly in respect of those literature reviews that have been conducted in a systematic and rigorous manner (Aveyard, 2010).

Types of Literature Review

The two main types of literature review you are likely to come across are:

- narrative literature reviews
- systematic literature reviews.

Narrative literature reviews

These are sometimes referred to as traditional literature reviews and are likely to be the most common type of literature review that you come across. They are characterised by a concern for drawing together conceptual and theoretical ideas from a range of literature. However, they can vary widely in terms of how explicit the reviewer is about how they:

- carried out the review process
- carried out their search strategy
- decided on what to include and exclude from their review
- decided on what to foreground in their synthesis of material.

In this sense, they are often viewed as being less rigorous than systematic reviews, but for students and novice literature review writers they are likely to represent the first stage of your literature review journey. They can also offer a greater degree of flexibility and the facility to adapt and change as the literature review progresses.

Systematic literature reviews

Systematic literature reviews are generally much more rigorous and systematic in terms of:

- how the review process is carried out
- how material is assessed or appraised
- how findings are reported.

They have effectively come to be seen as the 'gold standard' in respect of literature reviews.

The focus of systematic reviews is usually very well defined and relates to practice-based contexts and issues. They aim to address as much of the published literature as possible in order to develop a comprehensive coverage of the topic under investigation.

Systematic reviews require a high level of transparency relating to issues such as:

- how the research question was identified
- how the topic area was defined
- what data sources (e.g. particular databases) were used for searching
- the search terms and keywords used, and whether the search strategy was adapted or modified
- the extent of the literature identified through the search process
- the selection criteria used to decide which literature to include and exclude from the final study
- the method of the data extraction process (e.g. how data was taken from individual studies)
- the problems and challenges involved in synthesising findings/results from a number of different studies
- how consistency was maintained (this is particularly important in cases where reviews are carried out by teams).

As you can gather, the comprehensive and rigorous nature of systematic literature reviews means that they require a lot of skilful work and, in practice, are often carried out by small, dedicated teams of reviewers.

?   Did you know? Systematic review protocols   ?

Protocols are frameworks, used in the systematic review process, that are developed in advance of reviewers going off and finding the literature. Their purpose is:

- to ensure that the decision making that takes place is transparent – in this sense, they can function as a kind of audit trail
- to ensure both accuracy and consistency of approach in how the review is carried out

Review protocols are scrutinised by a panel of stakeholders, who are familiar with the topic under investigation. The panel would normally include service-users and carers (Macdonald, 2003: 5).

Have a look at the comparison table (Table 1.2), which summarises the key features and differences between narrative and systematic literature reviews.

Table 1.2   The key differences and features of narrative and systematic literature reviews

	Narrative Literature Reviews	Systematic Literature Reviews
Focus:	Tends to focus on analysing and synthesising conceptual and theoretical findings from a range of sources	Clear focus on appraising the quality of evidence encountered in the literature, often with a view to informing and improving practice outcomes
Explicitness of search strategy:	Often relatively undefined	Clearly defined and systematically applied
Comprehensiveness:	May offer wide coverage, but does not necessarily aspire to be comprehensive	Aims to be as exhaustive as possible
Decisions about inclusion/exclusion of material:	Can be selective and piecemeal	Clear protocol is devised to guide decision making about what is included and excluded
Potential for bias:	'Author(s)' decision-making process is often not explicit so there is scope for bias	Collaborative creation of protocol and transparent process tend to minimise potential for bias
Validity and reliability:	The lack of transparency about how the review has been carried out and the potential for *ad hoc* inclusion of material raises questions about the confidence that can be placed in the findings	Due to the systematic use of the protocol in all stages of the research, and the transparency with which review decisions are described, findings are likely to be valid and reliable
Key advantages:	Narrative reviews can be useful for synthesising ideas, theories and concepts from a broad range of literature	The systematic nature of this work means that it is of a high quality and is repeatable
Key disadvantages:	Quality can be variable, but in trying to assess the quality of narrative reviews one may be frustrated by a lack of transparency in respect of the review process	Although systematic reviews can be good at identifying 'what' works, they may not always be the most appropriate tool for identifying 'why' something works

Which type of review model should you adopt?

If you are carrying out a literature review for an assessment as part of a university-based social work course, it is unlikely that you will have the time, resources or experience to carry out a fully-fledged systematic review. However, as you will hopefully note from Table 1.2, there are aspects of narrative literature reviews that seem relatively weak or inconsistent in comparison to systematic reviews. So, with this in mind, we would tend towards a position outlined by Aveyard (2010: 16), which recommends that students aspire to the same levels of *transparency* required in a systematic review, while recognising that it is usually not possible to achieve the same level of comprehensive coverage.

If you are a social work practitioner or research student and you are preparing a literature review as groundwork for your own empirical study, then it would be useful to familiarise yourself more fully with the requirements for producing a systematic review. Even if you decide that it is not feasible to carry out a systematic review, the principles will help you to produce a more rigorous narrative review.

SCIE flowchart

To get a quick overview of the stages involved in carrying out a systematic review according to Social Care Institute for Excellence's guidelines, have a look at the 'Flowchart of systematic review process' in *SCIE Systematic Research Reviews: Guidelines* (Rutter et al., 2010: 10). This flowchart is also available at: www.scie.org.uk/publications/researchresources/rr01.asp
What do you think is the significance of each stage?

Methods Used in Literature Reviewing

Literature reviewing involves a number of different activities and processes, which become significant at different stages of the review process. The organisation of the chapters of this book broadly reflects the order in which you would normally carry out these activities and processes. Each activity will require the reviewer to make decisions about what particular methods to use.

Search methods

Searching for literature can involve multiple methods, such as:

- manual searching – searching by hand using paper-based journals
- electronic database searching – making use of multiple ways of searching fields and records
- keyword searches – experimenting with different combinations of words
- boolean operators – using special Boolean terms to alter the scope of the search
- developing, applying and revising exclusion and inclusion criteria.

It's likely that you will have come across many of these methods before in relation to literature searching that you will have done for other academic assignments. However, learning to be more structured and organised in the way that you carry out searches can take some practice. Chapter 4 contains some tips and advice to help you with this.

Data extraction methods

The purpose of data extraction is 'to extract the findings from each study in a consistent manner to enable later synthesis, and to extract information to enable quality appraisal so that the findings can be interpreted' (Rutter et al., 2010: 47). In other words, the data extraction process allows the reviewer to:

- pull out relevant findings and data from each of the selected studies
- compare, contrast and pull together findings where appropriate.

To do this, the literature reviewer must first identify what kinds of data are of interest, and then devise a consistent approach to identifying and extracting this data from the literature under review. This data may be either quantitative or qualitative, or a mixture of both.

For systematic literature reviews, it is common to use a special 'data extraction form', which aims to ensure that a consistent, objective and unbiased approach is taken. For the same reasons, the data extraction process may be undertaken by two or more reviewers. The *SCIE Systematic Research Reviews: Guidelines* (Rutter et al., 2010: 91–4) includes a sample data extraction form which outlines the kinds of information that may need to be recorded, including:

1. **Publication details** (e.g. author name, year of publication, title, etc.)
2. **Details about the nature of the study** (e.g. aims, questions addressed, site of research, target population, theories/models used, etc.)
3. **Details about the nature of practice interventions** (e.g. type and aim of intervention, practice setting, rationale, implementation issues, etc.)
4. **Outcomes and results** (e.g. how outcomes are measured, what the outcomes were, what the strengths/limitations of the study were).

Issues in data extraction

Although there are clearly many strengths to using such a detailed and systematic approach to data extraction, one of the potential challenges is that if the data extraction form is not designed appropriately, it may not always 'fit' or 'map' very closely the range of literature you are likely to come across. This may make the later stages of comparison and synthesis very difficult. So, unless you are completing a fully-fledged systematic review, you may need to adopt a more pragmatic and flexible approach to data extraction.

The ways in which quantitative data might be extracted from research papers and studies (essentially you are dealing with numerical and statistical data) may seem fairly obvious, but it is also possible to extract qualitative data in a consistent and systematic way. For instance, the SCIE report, *Using Qualitative Research in Systematic Reviews: Older People's Views of Hospital Discharge* (Fisher et al., 2006), provides an example of how a qualitative approach was used in the context of a systematic review. Other examples of the methodological issues involved in attempting to bring together insights and findings from a range of different research designs are provided in the report *Using Evidence from Diverse Research Designs* (Popay and Roen, 2003).

Critical appraisal methods

In appraising the literature you are aiming to:

- form a judgement about whether a particular publication is relevant to the topic of your literature review
- assess whether you think that the findings and implications are reliable and valid.

The focus of the critical appraisal is on the way in which the *research* has been carried out, as opposed to the effectiveness of any intervention reported on. Literature reviewers will often develop or adopt critical appraisal tools to assist them in carrying out a thorough and consistent appraisal process.

For your own literature review processes you will need to spend some time considering what kind of appraisal criteria are most appropriate to your review. Rutter et al. (2010) have identified some general issues that they would expect to be addressed in a systematic review appraisal tool for empirical studies. These include the following:

- Has the research been designed in such a way that can appropriately address the question?
- Did services users and carers have input into the design of the study?
- Was the research carried out in an ethical manner (e.g. with informed consent, etc.)?
- What kind of sampling method was used and was this appropriate for the study?
- Were all participants present throughout the study or did some discontinue? If so, what were the reasons for this?
- Were those involved in service/intervention delivery also involved in data collection and analysis?
- Have all the issues outlined at the outset of the study been addressed?
- Have the authors declared any interests (i.e. potential for gain or profit)?

Appraisal tools for qualitative studies are often developed specifically for the job in hand.

CASE STUDY

Devising appraisal criteria

For their worked example of a systematic review on older people's views of hospital discharge, Fisher et al. (2006) identify four markers that they used in assessing the quality of the papers that they accumulated through their searching process. These were:

1. **Strength of the research design** – how appropriate was the design for addressing the research questions that were identified?
2. **Centrality of older people's views** – this criterion reflects that aim of the study, which was to identify 'older people's own views and concepts, expressed in their own words, in accounts structured as they wished' (2006: 26).

3. **Quality of analysis and reporting** – was there sufficient depth and detail included in the papers to suggest confidence in the findings that were presented?
4. **Generalisability** – did the papers contain information in relation to the contextual factors which might impact on the study findings, and 'permit some generalisation beyond the immediate context in which the data were collected' (2006: 25)?

They then used a grid containing these four criteria to help them appraise the quality of the 15 studies they were focusing on.

We will return to this issue of critical appraisal in more detail in Chapter 6.

Methods for synthesis

Synthesis means 'bringing together', and in relation to literature reviews it describes the process of drawing together the data and findings from the literature in order to address or answer the review question. Table 1.3 provides a summary of some of the key synthesis methods, as identified by Rutter et al. (2010).

Table 1.3 Summary of the key synthesis methods identified by Rutter et al. (2010)

Method	Characteristics
Non-empirical studies method	– Relates to material which does not report on empirical studies, but which may contain information or perspectives useful for a literature review – Difficult to apply appraisal criteria to this, so general advice is to avoid treating such material as data or evidence
Statistical meta-analysis method	– Data from a number of studies are extracted and combined, allowing reviewers to carry out statistical analysis on this combined data – Allows broad generalisations to be made above the level of individual studies – Complex process, usually requiring the skills of an experienced statistician
Narrative synthesis method	– Concerned with establishing patterns and relationships between data – Seeks to assess the quality of the data – Reflects on the robustness of the synthesis process – Useful for working with diverse data
Qualitative data synthesis (QDS)	– Used with qualitative data – Common themes are identified across qualitative studies – Transparent, consistent approach differentiates it from 'narrative' synthesis method
Mixed methods synthesis	– Draws on a number of the other approaches – Synthesis is addressed from a number of perspectives – Can mitigate against limitations of any one particular method

Consider the case study below to see how one of these synthesis methods was applied in practice.

CASE STUDY

Qualitative Data Synthesis (QDS) in action

Fisher et al.'s (2006: 32–48) approach to synthesis was to use an 'interpretive' approach based on identifying and testing concepts across the studies they considered. They used a method of coding the data in order to clearly identify the themes and concepts that emerged from the individual studies. They then organised their coded data into three levels, as follows:

1. **Concepts/themes** – e.g. illness had an impact in making older people feel weak and tired
2. **Second-order concepts (interpretations)** – e.g. older people's capacity for assertiveness is undermined by physical dependency
3. **Third-order interpretations/hypotheses** – e.g. notions of expertise legitimate power.

Whichever method of synthesis is used, the intention should be to remain as transparent as possible about how it is being carried out, how consistency of approach is being ensured, and what the respective strengths and limitations of the method are.

Brief Anatomy of a Literature Review

Literature review length and structure

Literature reviews are usually quite substantial pieces of work, by which we mean they are normally longer than standard essays or assignments. One practical reason for this is that there is normally quite a lot to write about as you have (hopefully) taken a broad view of a topic, based on a reasonably comprehensive reading of the relevant literature. If you are completing a literature review as part of an academic course, you will be given clear guidance about how long the literature review should be.

Table 1.4   A typical literature review structure

Element	Function
Abstract/Summary/ Executive summary (approx. 250 words)	A brief overview of the key aspects of the literature review.
Introduction	Introduces the main topics and 'sets the scene' for the literature review.
Review methodology	Comments on the ways in which the review process was carried out. Considers searching, critical appraisal and synthesis, and any critical or methodological frameworks applied.
Literature review	The main body of the literature review, where the reviewer gets to grips with drawing out the main areas of discussion.

Element	Function
Discussion	The part where the reviewer discusses the significance, relevance and implications of what they have established in the literature review.
Conclusions	A summary of the literature review findings.
Reference list	A comprehensive, alphabetical list of all sources referred to in the literature review.

A typical literature review structure is shown in Table 1.4, although it's important to note that not all literature reviews will follow this format. There are often particular stipulations about how systematic reviews should be structured which may differ from this model (e.g. SCIE Systematic Reviews, Cochrane Reviews, etc.). If you are completing a review for an academic assignment, we would normally expect that you would be given specific guidance about the required structure.

We will cover the kinds of writing skills required to successfully complete each of these sections in Chapter 8.

Research Literacy

In order to review the literature successfully, you will need to be confident that you understand a few fundamental principles about how research is carried out within the social sciences. The reason for this is that a large proportion of the academic literature that you will be reading will be accounts of academic or practitioner-led research carried out within the health and social care field.

As a literature reviewer your job is not simply to read and digest this material (although this certainly forms part of the process). Instead, you will need to make critical and evaluative judgements about the methods, data, analysis, discussion and conclusions put forward by their respective authors. This is a challenging task at the best of times, but will be even trickier if you have not yet fully grasped some of the fundamental principles of research.

If you are an undergraduate or postgraduate social work student, you are likely to have studied research principles and methods by the time you come to undertake a literature review. However, if you have been out of education for some time, or are approaching literature reviews as a social work practitioner new to research, it would be worth reading a text such as *Research Skills for Social Work* by Andrew Whittaker (2009). As we progress through the book we will provide quick definitions and explanations of any specialist research jargon.

Ideas for Taking Things Further

1. Search for a research paper or article that is focused on the topic of your own literature review (or if this is not appropriate at this stage, choose a social work-related topic). Read it through and then have a go at applying Pawson et al.'s (2003) TAPUPAS criteria to test the quality of the evidence.

2. Read the SCIE report *Using Systematic Reviews to Improve Social Care* (Macdonald, 2003). It is only 21 pages long and will give you a thorough understanding of the nature of systematic reviews in social care.
3. For more discussion of some of the challenges of using systematic reviews in social care, read *Systematic Reviews: What Have They Got to Offer Evidence-based Policy and Practice?* (Boaz et al., 2002).

Going grey!

1. The piece of work aimed to draw together findings from smaller-scale research projects on drug prevention among young people and responses to local contexts that were not widely discussed in existing published work.

2. The researchers focused on grey literature because it has the potential to:
   i. give an up-to-date and detailed account of current drugs activity.
   ii. be more reflective of the fast-changing and locally influenced nature of drugs-related activity.
   iii. provide a greater level of detail about the process and implementation of policies and interventions.

3. The researchers proceeded by using four search strategies:
   i. Web searches (in particular, they cite online databases such as Mentor UK)
   ii. Consultation with professional networks (they specifically mention the National Collaborating Centre for Drug Prevention (NCCDP))
   iii. Consultation with Drug Action Teams
   iv. Specialist library and database searches (e.g. DrugScope, Web of Science, MEDLINE, and others).

4. The researchers used critical appraisal criteria so that only studies of relatively high quality (i.e. studies that were well designed and implemented) were examined and to weed out poor quality or poorly executed work.

5. Three limitations of the grey literature identified by the researchers were:
   i. Many projects were felt to rely on intuition rather than evidence of what works.
   ii. Some made reference to 'questionable' research evidence or approaches.
   iii. Indicators of success were based on arbitrary outcome variables, making it difficult to draw more general conclusions.

Chapter Summary

- We have considered the nature of knowledge and evidence in relation to social care knowledge and practice.
- We have explored what is meant by 'the literature' and have considered the nature and value of 'grey literature'.
- We have considered the different roles that a literature review typically performs, and have looked at the qualities and merits of narrative and systematic literature reviews.
- We have briefly looked at the different methodologies involved in carrying out a literature review.

Further Reading and Useful Resources

Aveyard, H. (2010) *Doing a Literature Review in Health and Social Care: A Practical Guide.* Maidenhead: Open University Press. (See Chapter 1, 'Why do a literature review in health and social care?', for additional reading about what literature reviews are and why they are useful in health and social care.)

Boaz, A., Ashby, D. and Young, K. (2002) *Systematic Reviews: What Have They Got to Offer Evidence-based Policy and Practice?* London: Economic and Social Research Council. (This academic paper considers the application of systematic reviews to social policy and practice, as well as the opportunities and challenges that this entails.)

Cochrane Collaboration Open Learning Material on Systematic Reviews available at: www.cochrane-net.org/openlearning/HTML/mod0.htm. (This online tutorial is designed to better equip those who are about to embark on a Cochrane systematic review. We suggest you might like to dip into various sections of it in order to gain a more in-depth understanding of what is required in the process of carrying out a systematic review.)

Gough, D., Oliver, S. and Thomas, J. (2012) *An Introduction to Systematic Reviews.* London: Sage. (This very detailed and comprehensive guide to systematic reviews addresses their use both in health and social care contexts.)

Ridley, D. (2008) *The Literature Review: A Step-by-Step Guide for Students.* London: Sage. (Although this book is not specifically focused on social work, Chapters 1 and 2 provide a broad and very readable introduction to what literature reviews are and why they are used.)

Whittaker, A. (2009) *Research Skills for Social Work.* Exeter: Learning Matters. (This book provides an overview of research skills for social work, and Chapter 2 provides a complete summary of the literature review process.)

The Research Mindedness website has been developed with funding from the Social Care Institute for Excellence (SCIE) in order to 'help students and practitioners of social care and social work make greater and more effective use of research in their studies and in practice' (SCIE/CHST, n.d.). It has been designed in such a way that you can dip in and out of sections that are most relevant to you. It can be accessed at: www.resmind.swap.ac.uk/index.htm (NB: Since 2005, this website has no longer been actively developed.)

References

Aveyard, H. (2010) *Doing a Literature Review in Health and Social Care: A Practical Guide.* Maidenhead: Open University Press.

Boaz, A., Ashby, D. and Young, K. (2002) *Systematic Reviews: What Have They Got to Offer Evidence-based Policy and Practice?* London: Economic and Social Research Council.

Fisher, M., Qureshi, H., Hardyman, W. and Homewood, J. (2006) *Using Qualitative Research in Systematic Reviews: Older People's Views of Hospital Discharge.* London: Social Care Institute for Excellence (SCIE).

Hart, C. (1998) *Doing a Literature Review.* London: Sage.

Hartman, K.A. (2006) 'Social policy resources for social work: grey literature and the internet', *Behavioural & Social Sciences Librarian,* 25(1): 1–11.

Hodson, H. and Cooke, E. (2004) 'Leading the drive for evidence-informed practice', *Journal of Integrated Care,* 12(1): 12–18.

Macdonald, G. (2003) *Using Systematic Reviews to Improve Social Care.* London: SCIE.

Pawson, R., Boaz, A., Grayson, L., Long, A. and Barnes, C. (2003) *Types and Quality of Knowledge in Social Care.* London: SCIE.

Popay, J. and Roen, K. (2003) *Using Evidence from Diverse Research Designs.* London: SCIE.

Rutter, D., Francis, J., Coren, E. and Fisher, M. (2010) *SCIE Systematic Research Reviews: Guidelines* (2nd edition). London: SCIE.

Schöpfel, J. (2010) 'Towards a Prague Definition of Grey Literature', *Proceedings of the Twelfth International Conference on Grey Literature: Transparency in Grey Literature.* Grey Tech Approaches to High Tech Issues, Prague, 6–7 December.

SCIE/CHST (n.d.) *Using This Resource* [Online]. Available at: www.resmind.swap.ac.uk/content/01_about/about_index.htm (accessed 16 June 2013).

Whittaker, A. (2009) *Research Skills for Social Work*. Exeter: Learning Matters.

2

Developing a
Research Topic

☑ **Learning Outcomes** ☑

- To clarify the choice of topic, working within the framework of your course of study or the specific purpose of your literature review for practice requirements
- To develop an understanding of your own knowledge, interests and/or specialism
- To see your topic in the wider context of published work in the chosen subject area and to develop clarity about the gaps in these areas of publication
- To be confident that your topic is refined to represent the exact area that you intend to research

---

Getting Started

You have a *long* read ahead of you as you start to identify the topic for your specific literature review. Indeed, some of this reading will take place as a part of the sifting process that you will go through, so the bad news is that some of the initial reading will not be directly used in your final piece of work. However, we are sure that this reading will expand your overview of the topic area and help with your overall view of the subject. It is always difficult to know when or if material will be useful and it is often with hindsight that we wish we had been more serious in the recording of notes from our reading, so it may be wise to make copious notes as you read and decide later on their relevance to your work.

It may be that the topic you choose is in an area of keen interest to you or that you are being directed to the topic through your course of study or your work setting. It is pertinent to consider just how much time you have to develop your topic and, more importantly, to complete the literature review.

The initial consideration of the topic will be influenced by the deadline that you need to meet for the submission of your finished work. In this respect, a time plan

will be of real benefit. It will help you to map out just how much time you can allocate for the initial reading to decide on your topic, and allow you to assess a realistic
time frame for the full task of completing your literature review.

It is relevant at this point to remind you of the note-taking skills that you will have
developed earlier in your studies. If you need more guidance on these specific skills,
we can recommend a good study skills text (Stogdon and Kiteley, 2010). Nepotism
at its worst!

How Much Choice Do You Really Have?

You may be studying on a qualifying/post-qualifying course in social work and may
be required to develop a research topic to meet the requirements of an assessed piece
of work as part of your course. In this situation, you may well be asked to develop
your literature review to consider the impact of a specific area of knowledge on the
understanding of social work practice. Or it may be that the literature review topic
is a purely academic exercise to support an academic piece of work that will be part
of the evidence of your ability to apply your knowledge and understanding of
research methodologies in a structured and directed way. Alternatively, you may be
a qualified social worker who is studying at a post-qualifying level and you are looking to identify a literature review topic for your Master's dissertation.

In both instances, your choice may be limited by your position. For example, as
a qualifying student on a qualifying course there may be some specific subject areas
that you will be asked to explore as part of the academic assignment requirements.
This may be defined by the service setting of your placement, if the topic of your
literature review needs to have a practice connection, and this in turn may be part
of the academic evidence in your practice portfolio. As a post-qualifying student you
may be funded by your employer, who has asked you to explore a specific subject
area that will inform your agency's understanding of a particular area of social work.

Before you begin your exploration and reading, it is important for you to be clear
about your own choice of topic and to establish some of the boundaries regarding
this choice that may be set by the demands of your course or employer. If you have
a completely free choice of topic, it may be worth thinking about whether the topic
you are considering is to fill a gap in your knowledge and understanding, or if you
have already developed some basic understanding of the subject but want to expand
this to a more detailed and sophisticated level. In a nutshell, what do you already
know about this subject area? You may have some knowledge from practice about
the topic, but have not explored this in an academic context.

Another consideration may be about whether you have had some direct experience of the topic in either a professional context or a personal one. If this is the
case, it may be sensible to reflect on how the study will impact on you, should you
go ahead. It may be that your own experiences have triggered your interest in the
specific subject area and that your hands-on experience will inform your approach
to the topic.

For example, if you have chosen to look at the impact of bullying on the social
development of young children, and this choice has been guided by your work with
children who have become very withdrawn following experiences of bullying, then
you may want to test out some of these individual observations within the wider

knowledge base in this subject area. You may want to examine this area of knowledge to remove the individualisation of bullying from the children involved and to try to gain a more in-depth understanding of why and how bullying behaviours are reproduced, with such far-reaching consequences for both the bully and the bullied. If you have reached this objective standpoint, you are demonstrating your understanding of the importance of an objective approach to your literature review and have started to think in a research-minded way that will undoubtedly be helpful as the starting point of your literature review. You may be on placement or employed in an educational setting in which the problem of bullying is an area that concerns children, parents and staff. If this is the case, then it may be worth pooling resources of existing knowledge by discussing your proposed topic for review with the people who are working with you in this area.

Alternatively, you could have experienced bullying personally, either as a child or an adult. If this is the case, your own subjectivity in regard to the topic will warrant a reflective approach, if only to establish if the area has had a personal impact on you in the past that may be relevant to your current understanding of the chosen topic for your literature review. As a discipline, social work understands the importance of reflection and the role it can play in the effectiveness of understanding. As such, it may be that you can identify how your personal experience can enhance but also potentially inhibit your understanding of your chosen topic for research.

Not a Student at All?

You may well need to access all the current literature in a given area as part of your day-to-day social work practice and not in the role of a student who is studying on a specific course. For example, you may be preparing a court report in care proceedings to demonstrate professional concerns about a child's safety in the family setting. The evidence that you present to the court will need to be measured and informed by credible theoretical knowledge. If, for example, you are asking the court to consider the effect on a child of being parented by parents who have a seriously chaotic lifestyle due to an unmanaged substance addiction, you will need to demonstrate how this level of care may be damaging to children. The risk needs to be clearly evidenced and this view will need to be supported by credible evidence (Munro, 2008). In this context, you will need to demonstrate that you have taken a measured and reasonable look at the literature that has examined the safety of children in similar situations. Commendably, this may be part of your whole approach to the evidence-based practice that social work aspires to in order to be recognised as a professional discipline that is informed by accredited knowledge and understanding.

Seeing Your Topic in a Wider Context

The validity and credibility of your work will start with the way that you approach the topic, and it will also depend on how serious you are prepared to be in the search for work that is already published in the specific area. As you begin to explore your topic you will be aware of the importance of checking the credibility and academic currency of the literature that you are reading. McLaughlin (2012) provides a clear guide to understanding and assessing the credibility of both quasi-experimental and qualitative studies.

Initially, you will need to look at the subject in both the narrowest and widest context. This will mean looking for the keywords that will help you to define your subject. If, for example, you plan to look at how you might begin to understand the published research in the area of 'child safeguarding', an important consideration will be to look at how this area has been researched, by whom and in which context the research has been undertaken.

In your initial searches you will need to consider the most appropriate terminology regarding your subject area. With regards to child safeguarding, this has a particular relevance in the light of the lessons learned from Serious Case Reviews, as recent writers have purposely moved away from the word 'safeguarding' towards the word 'protection', which has a historical context and is presented to emphasise the need to recognise the inherent risk involved when children are faced with caregivers who fail to protect them (NSPCC, 2011). The word 'protection' also portrays a clear role for professionals and their explicit duties to protect – the emphasis is much more overt than a concept of safeguarding, which has a more nebulous position in the understanding of professional roles.

Therefore, it is pertinent to consider how keywords and phrases will help you to define your topic in a more detailed way and to define the time span of the literature that you intend to review. In the case of child safeguarding/protection, there has been a wealth of literature in recent times, so, for example, you may want to define your search to a limited period, say from 1990 to the present day. Your choice to restrict the time span of your literature review will need to be explained in your introduction to the work, where you will have the opportunity to explain why you have chosen to look at a specific period in time.

Identifying the Gaps

The context

Research has informed the understanding and knowledge base for social work in relation to child safeguarding/protection and this has been contextualised in the high-profile cases that have made the headlines of both social work literature and the mainstream press (Munro, 2008). These cases are largely concerned with some very tragic circumstances, in which a child has died as a result of abusive care from a parent or caregiver. Many of the Serious Case Reviews (SCRs) have criticised the way that social work has intervened in these cases. Indeed, these criticisms have impacted upon the professional understanding of safeguarding/protection in a very direct way and have changed the way that social work is organised in relation to the safeguarding/protection of children. However, to rely only on where social work has gone wrong in the safeguarding/protection of children is only part of the equation, and we do need to consider some of the more innovative aspects of successful work which has taken place in the protection of children (Ferguson, 2011). Thus, the context of the starting point for your research will be to look both specifically at areas where social work has not been successful and at the same time consider the more rounded positions of where social work has successfully safeguarded/protected children (Ferguson, 2011). In this respect, the context for your literature review will need to include both historical and contemporary knowledge and understanding that published research has produced in this field.

Finding the work that has already been published

You have chosen child protection as the topic for your literature review but you now need to refine the topic to proceed with the specific area that you wish to examine.

Make a quick list of all the factors connected to child protection that you have come across, e.g. power, secrecy, communicating with children, poverty, politics and risk. Next, with each of the areas on the list, go into the electronic resources at your college/university library and identify three publications that are available in these areas. Ideally, the publications need to be peer-reviewed and to have been published in the last five years. Now summarise the key concepts in the works you have chosen.

Present your findings to your academic supervisor when you meet to discuss how your topic can be refined to a specific area of study for your literature review.

This activity will be one of the stages in the development of your research-mindedness and set you off on the route to the successful progress of your literature review.

ACTIVITY

Who has done the research?

Gathering a comprehensive list of the published work in your area of interest will give you an opening to understanding where the gaps are in relation to this subject.

The starting point for your search will be to locate and look at the most accessible work that has been published in your chosen topic. If we continue to explore safeguarding/protection, then that may be looking at research that has informed the policy and guidance on child well-being and safeguarding practice (DCSF, 2009). In the context of child safeguarding, you may go on to explore and examine some of the more subtle understandings that will inform how you contextualise the published work in this area. Looking at who has conducted research in one area may lead you to explore the interest and expertise of these published researchers. For example, if social work is the professional discipline of the researchers into the specifics of safeguarding/protection, it may be that the work leads on to other relevant areas of social work practice.

If this is the case, then you may want to explore if research around child safeguarding/protection has been inclusive of some of the key aspects of working effectively with children and their parents/caregivers. This may be through looking at the work done to establish the importance of effective communication between social workers and children in a safeguarding context. This is the start of refining your research topic. We will explore this in greater detail in the next section of this chapter.

Another important aspect of finding out exactly who has published research in your chosen area will be to develop your electronic research skills and also develop a positive working relationship with a knowledgeable and, in our experience, usually very interested and helpful librarian. At this stage you will be establishing the quality and relevance of published research, and subject specialist librarians have a specific expertise on the status of peer-reviewed research publications which will save you some considerable time – the hours wasted on the many conversational surfs of knowledge snapshots are both frustrating and distracting when you are trying to establish the credibility of sources at this point in your work. Your realisation and understanding of the credible published research, along with an awareness of where the gaps are in your specific area of interest, will be an asset to you in relation to both time management and clarity of your next steps.

When you discover the content of other work in your topic area it is also important to look at the style that has been used – you will come across other literature reviews which will give you some pointers about how you might construct your own piece of work in this field. The level of critical consideration of the information will inform your exploration and it may even be useful to look at the keywords and phrases that have been used in the published work as this may be a relevant guide for your own work.

Think about not only *who* has done the research, but also *who is paying* for it. One important aspect of exploring the published work is to consider how this research has been commissioned and supported, e.g. by funding for specific projects from central government or through other funding streams that have been accessed through competitive applications on a wider international scale. Who the people are who have undertaken the research and how has it been done are important considerations when looking at both the historical and more contemporary publications in your chosen area. It may be that an organisation with a particular bias (and this may be the government of the day) has commissioned research with the intention of gathering knowledge to support a particular viewpoint or policy, and although this obviously would be closely scrutinised through ethical considerations, it may raise questions for you about the objectivity and viability of the commission. From your perspective, the credibility of the funding and the governance of the existing research will be important considerations in the context of your own work.

Refining your topic

It is important that you think about how you might refine your topic for research and not be sidetracked into other routes along the way. As we discussed earlier, if other aspects of safeguarding/protection have a relevance (e.g. communication), do not be distracted down a route that focuses primarily on communication when your chosen focus is more specifically on child safeguarding/protection. However, if you consider some of the published research on the importance of communication is relevant, you may also want to find out how communication skills play a significant part both in direct work with service users and carers and in effective inter-professional dialogues. These communications have been identified as essential in the exchange of reliable and accurate information that plays a crucial role in the protection of vulnerable people (Ferguson, 2011).

Staying with the subject of child safeguarding/protection, you may want to find out about a specific area that has a particular relevance for you in your studies. For example, you may want to focus specifically on the impacts of race and racial understandings in the context of safeguarding children. There are some well-documented understandings about the importance of maintaining a methodical scrutiny of children, regardless of their race, class, ethnicity, etc. (Laming, 2003). The lessons learned emphasise the importance of social workers being confident to challenge parents regardless of the race and ethnic context. Refining your safeguarding/protection subject to include issues of race, ethnicity and class will not trim down the amount of material that you will have access to, but it will provide a more specific consideration of some of the important complexities that occur in this subject area.

? Did you know? Research-mindedness as a way of improving social work practice ?

Everitt et al. (1992), cited in McLaughlin (2012: 11), identify three principles of research-mindedness that improve social work practice:

- A participatory/developmental approach is better than a social control model of social work.
- Anti-oppressive values should always be applied.
- Genuine partnerships are established with those whom social work serves.

Think about... Has your own practice to date been influenced by a specific piece of research?

Whether you have worked in child or adult protection, or in any other field, can you identify a piece of writing or research that has made you rethink a particular area of your practice?

Chapter Summary

- We have emphasised the importance of reading around your choice of topic before deciding on the specific title of your literature review.
- We have explored the importance of seeing the topic in a wider context and looking at the academic credibility of the literature reviewed.
- We have considered the importance of refining your topic and ensuring that your reading keeps you focused on the subject area that you have chosen to review.

- We have considered ways of identifying the gaps in these areas of publication.
- We have considered some examples from the field of child safeguarding/protection.

Further Reading and Useful Resources

Fish, S., Munro, E. and Bairstow, S. (2008) *Learning Together to Safeguard Children: Developing a Multi-Agency Systems Approach for Case Reviews*. London: SCIE. (This report provides useful context for the example topic of child safeguarding/protection referred to throughout this chapter.)

References

Department for Children, Schools and Families (DCSF) (2009) *Common Assessment Framework*. London: DCSF. Available at: www.education.gov.uk/childrenandyoungpeople/strategy/integratedworking/caf (accessed 13 March 2013).

Ferguson, H. (2011) *Child Protection Practice*. Basingstoke: Palgrave Macmillan.

Laming, Lord (2003) *The Victoria Climbie Inquiry*. Norwich: The Stationery Office.

McLaughlin, H. (2012) *Understanding Social Work Research* (2nd edition). London: Sage.

Munro, E. (2008) *Effective Child Protection* (2nd edition). London: Sage.

NSPCC (2011) A Summary of Ofsted's *The Voice of the Child: Learning Lessons from Serious Case Reviews*. London: NSPCC. Available at: www.nspcc.org.uk/inform/research/briefings/voice_of_the_child_wda81898.html (accessed 3 June 2013).

Stogdon, C. and Kiteley, K. (2010) *Study Skills for Social Workers*. Sage Study Skills Series. London: Sage.

3

Planning and Organising Your Literature Review

☑ Learning Outcomes ☑

- To understand how to use your time wisely
- To recognise the importance of setting goals and milestones
- To appreciate the use of Gantt charts and planning tools
- To identify study spaces and research resources
- To develop your understanding of project supervision

Using Your Time Wisely

Procrastination is the thief of time. (Proverb)

Procrastination, the act of needlessly delaying tasks to the point of experiencing subjective discomfort. (Solomon and Rothburn, 1984)

Need we go on? The reasons for *not* getting started can often be drawn up into a long list that, although detailed, may not always be convincing or credible and may (dare we say it?) sound like excuses rather than reasons for delay. You may be someone who has an accurate self-knowledge about how you manage your time, or you may not. In this chapter, we want you to build on your own understanding of using your time wisely and will offer some guidance about the strategies that can help you to enhance the management of your time in relation to the specific task of completing your literature review. Some helpful tips on time management, including goal setting, prioritising, dealing with worst first, forward planning and thinking ahead, can be found at www.successfulacademic.com/success_tips/Manage_time_organize.htm.

We do not want to assume that you lack organisational skills, and in the following quote it may be that the authors are saying more about themselves than about you, but we did find this message from the above source especially pertinent:

> If you spend more than five minutes a day searching for the things you need, then your disorganisation is interfering with your productivity.

We stand guilty as charged!

We do not want to underestimate the likely demands on your time. We assume that, as either an undergraduate or postgraduate social work student, you will most likely have a busy life outside the requirements of your academic course. We also know that you may not always be in control of the demands on your time – why does the car break down on your way to the library when you had planned a full day for research? Why is it that a child develops a high temperature and ear infection on the morning of the day that you have planned to make a start on the literature review as the submission date is scarily creeping closer and closer? We know that some situations will mean that you have to reschedule your study time and respond to other needs. But we would urge you to look at how easily you rejig your day, and to consider whether there are opportunities to draw in favours and maybe reduce the study time to half a day rather than the full one that you had planned. Friends or family may be willing to help but, in the absence of psychic powers, they do need to be asked! Or it may be your ability (or inability) to say 'no' that keeps you from making a start. The skill of assertion, which is so often required in social work practice, may not necessarily be one that you feel at ease with when using it to meet your own needs for study time.

It is perhaps relevant to explore just how effective you can be in securing the time that you need to sit down to plan and organise your literature review.

ACTIVITY

'How Assertive Are You?'

The Assertiveness Quiz – Stress Management – About.com (http://stress.about.com/library/assertiveness_quiz/bl_assertiveness_quiz.htm) is a really useful website that offers some key guidance on how assertiveness can help you manage your time and enable you to concentrate and prioritise your work on your literature review. The questionnaire on the website will give the opportunity to assess just how assertive you are and perhaps help you to identify areas that you need to address in order to assert your own needs rather than prioritise the needs of others.

Some of the key questions that are asked are:

- How can you avoid being overloaded by agreeing to requests from others that are impractical, if not impossible, for you to achieve?
- How can you reduce conflict when you have to say 'no' and also maintain a calm approach that diminishes the stress that may be felt through the refusal?

Go to the website above and follow the questionnaire to find out just how assertive you are.

Let us assume that you have conquered all the hurdles and distractions and now have some uninterrupted time to plan how you will best use the time available to you.

Think about... How much time have you really got?

- Think about your planning and organisation.
- Think about your timescales.
- Think about where to start looking for research sources.

Getting organised

You are a final-year undergraduate social work student and have to submit your literature review on 1 July 2014 and today's date is 1 January 2014. The subject topic that you are considering for your literature review is: 'The Role of Supervision in Child Protection Social Work Practice'.

For this activity we want you to quickly jot down some of the first thoughts you have about the task ahead of you. Remember that the focused task of your literature review is to look critically and analytically at the range of theories, research findings, books, journals, articles and reports, and to discuss how they have contributed to knowledge of the specific subject.

- Do you have any quick thoughts about the dates of the publications?
- Have you considered international perspectives?
- Is the publication peer reviewed?
- Is your list one that you could take to your first meeting with your academic supervisor to discuss your literature review?
- Do you have any thoughts on how you might start to extend/refine your search in the context of your subject topic?

Setting Goals and Milestones

As a student on a professional social work course, whether it is a qualifying or post-qualifying one, you will be acutely aware that the deadlines for the completion of your literature review will have been decided by someone other than you. This may be your tutor, course leader or employer, and they may have allocated a specific amount of time for you to complete your studies before resuming your full caseload again. (The cynics in us assume that it is very likely that you have not had significant time or workload relief to complete your studies, but perhaps we should guard against such a pessimistic stance?)

The demands on your time, whether from employment, academic study, personal commitments or all three, will impact on the goal setting for your literature review. It is important that the goals that you plan and the timescale you set for them are both practical and achievable. You will no doubt have looked at the basic guidance on goals, and indeed may have drawn upon the value of goal setting in your day-to-day practice with service users. You will find guidance on both goal setting and achievement in the task-centred approaches as defined by Teater (2010).

The popular goal-setting intervention in social work practice has been established with the Task-Centred Model, which concentrates on alleviating specific problems experienced by service users within a defined timescale and uses goal setting as a key factor (Reid and Epstein, 1972; Tolson et al., 2009). Task-centred work is defined by Reid and Epstein as 'a short-term, problem-solving approach and may be useful in work with both individuals and groups' (cited in Teater, 2010: 182–3). This approach offers a problem-solving structure that you may find has a specific application for you when you are setting the goals and milestones to complete the work on your literature review.

The basic components of task-centred work offer the opportunity to identify the problem and establish goals to solve the problem. This approach allows a clear appraisal of the tasks to be addressed and starts by defining the tasks. Once defined, the tasks are then allocated and this involves both the service user and the social worker deciding the tasks that they will each complete to ensure that the goals are achieved. The task-centred approach also requires a definite timescale in which the tasks can be completed. The emphasis of this intervention is both to give the service user control over their particular circumstance and to enable the social worker and the service user to work in partnership to enable the process of change that has been agreed.

A significant part of the task-centred process is to identify the tasks that are needed to reach the goals. The tasks are established as appropriate problem-solving activities and it is the completion of the tasks that will lead to the successful realisation of the goals.

It may seem pessimistic to identify the challenge of delays in completing your literature review as a problem, but, given the demands on your time, this may be an apt description. In the task-centred framework, if we think:

The problem is: DELAY IN WORKING ON YOUR LITERATURE REVIEW

The goal is: GETTING ON TRACK TO COMPLETE THE LITERATURE REVIEW

then the tasks associated with the successful achievement of the goal (to enable the completion of the literature review within the deadline for submission) may be defined as:

To find out what has already been researched on your chosen subject

To identify any sub-areas that need to be considered

To find out about other research that may connect to your subject area

To discover how the direct and associated areas of research in your subject all connect to each other

To identify your sources

To decide on the timescale for the above activities

The Reading University website (www.reading.ac.uk/internal/studyadvice/StudyResources/Essays/sta-startinglitreview.aspx) provides more detail on task-centred frameworks and offers suggestions as to how you might develop tasks in relation to your own specific subject area. But the key challenge here is to look at how much time you can allocate to working on the activities to complete the tasks and realise the goal of completing your literature review.

Planning Your Time

In previous chapters we have looked at how you will develop your understanding of the structures of literature reviews. We have also looked at how you develop the subject of your research topic. Now we have explored how the setting of goals and milestones will help with the planning and organisation of your literature review. The main focus of your work on your literature review will be the gathering of published literature, which you will then need to summarise and synthesise in the context of providing supporting evidence for the different perspectives that you have presented in your review. The key to the academic credibility of your literature review will be how rigorously you have sought to establish the supporting evidence, and the extent to which you have ensured that you have comprehensively considered the relevant views on your chosen topic. Knowing how much literature you need to review and how much evidence is needed to support the discussion will give you a guide as to the time you need in both the planning and organising stages of your piece of work. It is useful to look at how other disciplines have developed methods of planning to assist the successful achievement of a specific piece of work.

'Gantt' and 'CPM' (Critical Path Method) may be new terms to you as a social worker, but these concepts are very common in the world of project management. Over the next few pages we will look at both these concepts, although with the caveat that these tools are suggested as possible ways that may be useful to help you plan and organise your work schedule for your literature review. We are not prescribing them as useful for everyone and it may even be that the distraction of looking at project management techniques is enough to refocus you on the task in hand.

Gantt Charts

If you decide to use the Gantt chart, the importance of looking at the timescale of other associated activities involved in your literature review will become apparent. Understanding that some tasks will take place alongside others, or may only be achieved if certain conditions are met, is an important aspect of how you will perceive and use the time available to you.

Gantt charts have had a historical significance in project planning since their creation and consist simply of a bar chart to illustrate a project schedule. However, 'simply' may seem like an understatement if you log on to the following website: www.smartsheet.com/. What are your first thoughts on this website? The website provides a quick introduction to Gantt charts but the graphics may make you feel as if there is another force in front of you. There is! The complexity of the moving figures may make you question why we are directing you to charts that clearly connect to projects a long way from your literature review, but stay patient and proceed to this website: www.ganto.com

ACTIVITY

Here you will find a clear introduction to the Gantt chart. It describes how a bar chart is used to show the project schedule and provides a breakdown of the details of work that form the structure of the project. The breakdown of these details is referred to as the Work Breakdown Structure (WBS). The tasks associated with the structure of the project are detailed, along with a view as to how they influence the pace of the progress of the project. The way that the tasks interconnect and how they influence the progress of a project is also described. Because Gantt charts are more concerned with the management of the schedule, they do not address the overall size of the elements of work, as Morris (1994) explores.

Key elements of the Gantt chart are:

- activity – the activities you need to complete to achieve your goal
- predecessors – the other factors that need to be considered in addition to your project tasks
- time estimates – how long each activity will take
- expected time – the final submission date.

In drawing on the Gantt chart as an aide to your work on your literature review, we are using it in a very broad and personalised way. Indeed, in the world of project management theory there is very little recognition of some of the personal factors that can legitimately take over our time and attention. In asking you to look at the work as a process, we hope that you will be able to go easy on yourself when other demands overtake you and that you will not lose the energy to continue with the work on your literature review. As a social work student or a social worker, you will have explored the importance of self-awareness, emotional intelligence and resilience, all of which may provide a helpful insight and have a significant part to play in the planning and organisation of your literature review. The intention is to help you to look at the scope and breadth of the work that you have to complete and to recognise some of the hurdles that you may encounter, regardless of how well intentioned you are at the start of the process.

ACTIVITY

Applying Gantt charts to your literature review

The Gantt chart will give you the opportunity to draw a visual guide to the tasks that you will need to address in order to complete your literature review:

- **Activities** will include tasks associated with preparation, choosing the topic, searching resources, reading and note-taking, project supervision and writing up the work.
- **Predecessors** will be the areas of your work/personal time demands that may be relevant for you at the point of undertaking your literature review.
- **Time estimates** will be the plan of time you envisage each activity will take.
- **Expected time** will be the date of your final submission of your literature review.

Activities – Make a list of the activities that need to be undertaken to complete your literature review.

Time – Consider a timescale that gives you leeway and flexibility, but still meets your deadline requirements.

When, where and how?

There are several questions you need to consider before you begin your literature review:

- When will you start your research?
- Where will you work?
- How much do you know already?
- What are the sources that you plan to access?

Predecessors – Which factors will need to be considered alongside your plan to start your research? Do you have employment commitments that will impact directly on the activities that you have planned? Do you have childcare or caring commitments that will impact on the same plans?

Time estimates – How long do you envisage you will spend *going through* the activities list that you have drawn up? Think about a timescale in the light of you receiving all the support that you need to address the possible distractions, e.g. employment, childcare/caring responsibilities.

Critical Path Method (CPM)

Another aide to planning your time and organising your work for your literature review may be the Critical Path Method (CPM). Initially developed by Woolf (2007) as a commonly used and multidisciplined method of project modelling (although it is no longer used in its original form), it is still regarded by some to have currency as a method of mathematical analysis in relation to project planning. It is described as 'an algorithm', but don't glaze over if mathematics is the pinnacle of your own personal nemesis. The basic technique, as defined by Woolf (2007), is to construct a model that includes the following steps:

1 List all the activities required to complete the project.
2 Decide on the amount of time needed for each activity.
3 Examine and understand how the different activities depend on each other.

So let's look at how you might use this model with regard to planning and organising your literature review. We can do this by focusing on a specific subject and looking at how we will plan and organise the literature review in this area.

Let us suppose that the topic you have chosen for your literature review is focused on:

'The over-representation of young black men in restrictive mental health services in the UK'

1 Listing the activities to be completed

With the Critical Path Method in mind, let us start by identifying the first activity that you may choose to think about.

Finding out about the breadth and depth of the topic will involve looking at existing research on your topic. You will also need to examine any areas of research and publications that relate indirectly to your topic. So it may be useful to describe your first activity as setting the context for your study by establishing the source of your question in relation to the proportion of black British men in mental health services. To establish this context, your starting activity may be to examine online tools such as search engines, but avoid unnecessary expeditions with a general Google enquiry. The advice from the University of Reading is to concentrate on established works with academic credibility, such as books, journals, research reports and government publications.

Whichever resources you start with, you will need to visit the library. So, in relation to the CPM, you have two interconnected activities. The first one is finding the breadth and depth of your topic and the second is visiting the library to achieve this understanding.

2 Deciding on the amount of time needed for each activity

Can we suggest that you have some serious library time ahead of you? You may also want to cast your net across professional psychiatric publications as well as Home Office statistics to enable you to establish the all-important context of your chosen topic area. Remember that along with the searching, you will be doing a lot of reading and sifting, so let's be bold and allocate several hours – shall we say five days?

3 Examining and understanding how the different activities depend on each other

Still with the Critical Path Method in mind, think about how finding the depth and breadth of your topic will be dependent on you visiting the library. You have allocated a timescale to complete the two activities, but if you are unable to spend the time you have allocated, then the critical path that could lead to successfully completing the activities may be well and truly blocked. Hence, the relationship between looking at the breadth and depth and visiting the library is interdependent, and a recognition of this will give you the timescales that are possible (i.e. the shortest), but more likely the one that is probable (the longest).

Finding a Space to Study and Produce Your Finest Work!

Finding a suitable place to study is not just about locating the physical spaces where you can concentrate and hopefully not be interrupted. It is also about trying to maximise the opportunities for study as they arise. As a student on placement or as an employment-based student on a post-qualifying course, it may be that you have access to work-based or placement spaces to develop your literature review. We assume (hopefully not too cynically) that you will at times be burning the midnight oil while working on your review, and that you will also be working for some of your time in the university/college/workplace library. We want to explore with you the availability of your own 'head-space' for study, and also to look at how you might create the opportunity to have some quiet thinking time to read and consider the material that you have selected to include in your literature review.

The way that you decide to allocate your time for study will be enhanced with a clear plan and it may be useful to think about the benefits of using Gantt charts or taking a task-centred approach. We also suggest that the physical space may be more easily achievable than the emotional space, especially if you are engaged in social work practice, whether it is in employment or on a placement.

Some of the pitfalls to avoid, if your physical space permits the choice, are as follows:

- Try not to monopolise the dining table – your nearest and dearest may be well aware that you are studying and possibly feeling quite stressed without a daily reminder that they need to eat meals off their laps.
- If at all possible, choose a space where you can leave papers out, but, if not, try to file your papers in a simple way that means you can pick up where you left off when you resume your studies – we are very familiar with the frustrations of trying to locate the last point of work and having to backtrack unnecessarily – or maybe that's just us?
- If you are on placement and the work for literature review relates to the practice that you are undertaking, it may be that there will be opportunities to do some research as part of your placement study time (we know this is not always readily available, but it does happen for some lucky ones). If it is the case that you do have this opportunity, then your research for your review will be located in the practice setting – so make the most of it. You will be working alongside practitioners of all levels who may have very relevant information about particular publications that inform their practice, so, again, make the most of this opportunity.

When you have decided upon the space(s) that will be most productive for your study, it is important to be confident about how you will access the appropriate resources for your literature review. If you are using a university library, you will have access to a comprehensive range of research sources that will include both electronic and hard copies of books, journals and research papers. Your confidence with the use of the research sources will be influenced by the ease that you feel when using the library, either on campus or electronically from another place. The context of either placement or employment setting is again important as it is very likely that you will have access to electronic sources from the agency base. Other useful research sources will be in the form of literature reviews that have been done by past students, and these are usually available within the university library. It is unlikely that these sources will be available for loan, but access within the library is often a routine part of the services offered to students.

A search engine that is used by some universities is Summon (www.serialsolutions. com/en/services/summon), and it is really important that you feel confident to use this source in a way that is both focused and economical (with the limited time that you have available to you for this work).

Project supervision

> **? Did you know? There is a connection between supervision in social work and academic supervision ?**
>
> The qualities that make a good academic supervisor are:
>
> An ability to listen
>
> Knowledge of the subject area
>
> A critical approach to knowledge and practice
>
> Realism in timescales
>
> Being stimulating and conveying enthusiasm for research
>
> (Culen et al., 1994, cited in Delany, n.d.)

For most social workers, the term 'supervision' will represent a structure in which workload and resources are key features. Professional and personal development may be addressed but the main function remains the accountability of practice and the appropriate allocation of resources. However, Ferguson (2011) argues that supervision that supports the social worker to manage the anxieties of both their own feelings and the feelings of the service user can be an aide to clear and focused social work practice:

> Workers need containment of their own feelings and those projected on them by service users (and also by other professional colleagues) if they are to think clearly and keep their focus on the child. (Ferguson, 2011: 198)

The recognition that managing anxieties can lead to clarity and more focused social work practice may have a particular relevance to you, and also to how you will approach your own academic supervisor of your literature review. Bear in mind that the person appointed to be the supervisor of your work on your literature review may not be a social worker and, as such, will regard supervision in purely academic terms rather than in practice terms. It is important to recognise that academic supervision is very different from practice supervision.

The emphasis of your literature review supervisor will initially be on the credibility of the research sources that you plan to explore and also on supporting you in the given timescale for the completion of your work. It is important for both you and your supervisor to establish your expectations at the outset, and to have a clear definition of the roles and responsibilities for each of you.

It may be helpful to you as the student to look at some of the tasks that your supervisor may prioritise in the assessment of your work on your literature review. For example:

- to encourage the understanding of the primary objective of the literature review
- to help you to realise that the literature review is not merely a summary
- to ensure you understand the implications of academic plagiarism
- to ensure that you use resources that are academically credible and have peer-reviewed status
- to help you to use up-to-date research that has been rigorously analysed and critiqued (Chan, 2009).

Chapter Summary

- We have considered how you can use your time wisely and to good effect.
- We have examined how to develop your organisational skills to keep you on track in your research project.
- We have seen how using techniques such as Gantt charts and the Critical Path Method can help to get you started and keep you focused.
- We have examined how to set goals – and reach them!
- We have looked at project supervision.

Further Reading and Useful Resources

Bogo, M. and McKnight, K. (2006) 'Clinical supervision in social work', *The Journal of Clinical Supervision*, 24(1–6): 49–67. (This journal article is not only useful for its focus on supervision within social work, but is itself an example of a literature review.)

King, S. (1999) *On Writing: A Memoir of the Craft*. London: Hodder. (In part a memoir, as well as a guide to the practical aspects of writing (mainly fiction), by the celebrated novelist Stephen King.)

www.reading.ac.uk/internal/studyadvice/Study-resources/Essays/sta-startinglitreview.aspx (This web guide, from the University of Reading, provides a helpful overview of the literature review process.)

www.smartsheet.com/ (This is a website for a commercial software product used for time management and the creation of Gantt charts.)

If you decide to look further into the context of supervision in social work, the following article may be useful as it looks at the context and definitions of supervision in social work: http://infed.org/mobi/the-functions-of-supervision

References

Chan, C. (2009) *Assessment: Literature Review, Assessment Resources @ HKU*. Hong Kong: University of Hong Kong. Available at: http://ar.cetl.hku.hk (accessed 17 December 2012).

Delany, D. (n.d.) Centre for Academic Practice and Student. Available at: www.tcd.ie/CAPSL/assests/doc/Effective_Supervision_Literature_Review.doc (accessed 12 December 2012).

Ferguson, H. (2011) *Child Protection Practice*. Basingstoke: Palgrave Macmillan.

Morris, P.W. (1994) *The Management of Projects*. London: Thomas Telford.

Reid, W.J. and Epstein, L. (1972) *Task-Centred Casework*. New York: Columbia University Press.

Solomon, L.J. and Rothburn, E.D. (1984) 'Academic procrastination: frequency and cognitive-behavioural correlates', *Journal of Counselling Psychology*, 31(4): 503.

Teater, B. (2010) *An Introduction to Applying Social Work Theories and Methods*. Maidenhead: Open University Press.

Tolson, E., Reid, W.J. and Garvin, G. (2009) *Task-centred Practice: A Generalist Approach.* New York: Columbia University Press.

Woolf, M.B. (2007) *Faster Construction Projects with BPM Scheduling.* Maidenhead: McGraw Hill.

4

Literature Searching

☑ **Learning Outcomes** ☑

- To explore a four-stage process of literature searching
- To be able to identify the tools that can assist in generating keywords
- To be able to identify a range of useful literature (including grey literature) using databases, catalogues and websites
- To appreciate the usefulness of advanced search options, Boolean operators and phrase searching

Laying the Foundations of Your Literature Review

Think about... What are the foundations of a good literature review?

The success of this literature search process is a key component of the overall quality of the literature review (e.g. Grayson & Gomersall, 2003) and therefore any scholarly product flowing from the literature review. (Holden et al., 2008: 487)

The quality of your literature review will be largely determined by the scope, thoroughness and relevance of the material you dig up in your literature searching. Consequently, searching for relevant material will initially make up the bulk of your work in the early stages of the literature review process. Until you have done this, you don't really have anything to review!

Successful Searching in Four Stages

It can be helpful to break the literature search down into four separate stages:

1. **Identify search criteria** that are relevant to your topic.
2. **Search resources,** including databases, library catalogues and search engines.
3. **Access and evaluate** – acquire material through the searches you carry out and make a preliminary evaluation of its usefulness.
4. **Record and review** – reflect on your materials and your literature search process.

You will find that you may return to previous stages several times during the searching process. In fact, this is an indication that the search strategy is being modified and refined as the search progresses.

1 Identify Search Criteria

When you begin the search process you need to establish what your search criteria are, based on the literature review topic that you have identified. In particular, you need to think about where the boundaries of your search may lie (e.g. is it UK-focused? Which client group is it focused on? And so on). Your search criteria will in turn impact on the choice and combination of keywords that you use to interrogate databases, catalogues and search engines. It's likely that your search criteria will continue to emerge and develop as the search progresses, and it's worth noting that you shouldn't be too rigid about this in the early stages, as you may exclude material which could potentially be of use.

Think about... Keyword tools

Tools that can help you in the identification of keywords include:

- Dictionaries (either hard copy or online) for:
  - checking spellings
  - understanding precisely what terms mean
  - checking subject-specialist terminology using specialist dictionaries such as *Dictionary of Social Work* (Pierson and Thomas, 2010) or *The Blackwell Dictionary of Social Policy* (Alcock et al., 2002)
- Thesauri (either hard copy or online) for:
  - finding alternative words that have the same or similar meaning (known as synonyms)
- Keyword lists – journal articles (and some book chapters) will often contain a list of keywords which summarise the main aspects of the work. You can try these keywords out on your own searches.

Generating alternative search terms/keywords

To gain a clearer understanding of how the resources that you discover can help you to extend and modify your keywords, let's take a look at a specific case study.

Collecting keywords

Alice is conducting a literature review on service delivery for trafficked children in the United Kingdom, and begins her search using the keywords '**children**', '**trafficking**' and '**services**'.

Her results lead her to an article in the *British Journal of Social Work* entitled 'Working with trafficked children and young people' (Pearce, 2011). Alice notices that the journal article is described by a set of keywords (see below), which gave her many more ideas about the variations of keywords that she could use in her own searches.

Keywords: asylum seekers, child safeguarding, child protection, refugees, trafficking of children and young people, internal trafficking, child smuggling, child sexual exploitation, separated children, unaccompanied asylum-seeking children, missing children

---

Table 4.1 highlights some of the issues relating to language and terminology which are useful to think through when attempting to identify helpful keywords.

Table 4.1 Issues to consider when generating keywords

Issue	Example
Synonyms (words meaning same or similar things)	'children' could be described as 'young people', 'adolescents', 'youth', and so on
International differences	'domestic violence' is a common term in the UK and the USA, whereas 'intimate partner violence' is used more often in the USA than in the UK
General/specific	'services' can be more specifically described as 'social services', 'child protection services', and so on
Related topics	'child trafficking' may also be associated with child sexual exploitation, separated children, unaccompanied asylum-seeking children and missing children
Singular/plural	child, child's, children
Acronyms	cognitive behavioural therapy (CBT)

There are some special ways of inputting your keywords into online search engines and databases, which are particular 'wildcard' or 'truncation' characters, to help make your searching more efficient. The following box explains how and why you would do this, using specific examples.

> ### **? Did you know? Go Wild! – Wildcard and truncation searching ?**
>
> In cases where you may want to search using a term which has multiple forms (e.g. to indicate singular or plural forms), such as 'woman' or 'women', you can use the **wildcard** character '?' in place of the varying character. So, searching for 'wom?n' should pick up results containing 'woman', 'women' or even 'womyn' (one of several alternative spellings sometimes used in feminist work and writing).
>
> In cases where one of your keywords might have many different endings, such as child, child's, children, childcare, etc., it is possible to do a **truncation** search which should pick up all the possible variations. To do this, you simply type the wildcard character (in this case, it is an asterisk,'*') after the root part of your keyword. So, in this example, we would type the following into the search box:
>
> SEARCH: child*

2 Search Resources

Successful searching requires:

1. Knowing where to search
2. Knowing how to modify and adapt your search options

Knowing where to search

Academic institutions subscribe to a range of resources and they often provide some form of search engine to allow students and academics to search across the whole range of materials that can potentially be accessed. Similarly, social work employers will provide access to databases and information resources relating to professional practice, legal issues, and so on. Table 4.2 lists some of the databases, portals, catalogues and websites that will help you to find relevant resources.

Databases

At our own institution we use a service called Summon, developed by Serial Solutions, which allows users to search across a library's entire range of online and hard-copy material using one simple search facility. Some institutions will use similar services and some have even developed their own in-house systems.

Table 4.2 Resources for identifying literature

Resource name	a. Subject area / b. Type of resource	Web address	Brief guidance notes
ASSIA (Applied Social Sciences Index & Abstracts)	a. Social sciences / b. Subscription database	Online but requires subscription (check if you have access with your institution or employer)	Subscription database covering social science subjects, including social work. Contains in excess of 375,000 records from over 500 journals, including those from the UK and the USA.
CINAHL (Cumulative Index to Nursing and Allied Health Literature)	a. Nursing/health care / b. Subscription database	Online but requires subscription (check if you have access with your institution or employer)	Subscription database which covers nursing and allied health literature. You may be able to access it as part of your institution's library resources (if applicable), using an Athens password. Alternatively, you may be able to access it using your employer's access to e-resources.
Community Care Inform	a. Social care / b. Online database	www.ccinform.co.uk/home/default.aspx	Provides access to a range of social care-related content, including grey literature such as reference manuals, guides, resources and tools.
Department of Health – Publications and letters library search	a. Health & social care / b. Online database	http://webarchive.national archives.gov.uk/+dh.gov.uk/en/publicationsandstatistics/publications/publicationslibrary/index.htm	Allows users to search for publications, letters, circulars and related documents that have not been archived. Covers whole range of health and social care topics, including formally published documents and grey literature.
EPPI-Centre Evidence Library	a. Education, public health, social welfare and international development / b. Online database/library	http://eppi.ioe.ac.uk/	Provides access to the systematic reviews of research evidence carried out by the Evidence for Policy and Practice Information and Co-ordinating Centre (EPPI-Centre). These systematic reviews cover a number of subject areas, including social policy and welfare. The EPPI-Centre websites also contain resources for those conducting systematic reviews.
EThOs (Electronic Theses Online Service)	a. General / b. Online database	http://ethos.bl.uk/Home.do	Allows users to search all theses produced within UK higher education. In most cases an abstract is available, and in some instances it is possible to download a free electronic version of the full theses.

(Continued)

Table 4.2 (Continued)

Resource name	a. Subject area b. Type of resource	Web address	Brief guidance notes
Explore the British Library	a. General b. Online library catalogue	www.bl.uk/	Online catalogue of all publications published in the UK. Some of these may be ordered through inter-library loan services, or may be consulted at the British Library Reading Rooms at St Pancras, London or Boston Spa, West Yorkshire.
Intute: Social Sciences	a. Social sciences b. Subject specialist portal	www.intute.ac.uk/socialsciences/	Contains quality-assessed materials, including grey literature, geared towards the needs of students studying in the social sciences (NB: At the time of publication this resource is available but not being developed or maintained due to the withdrawal of funding).
NHS Evidence in Health and Social Care	a. Health & social care b. Subject specialist portal	www.evidence.nhs.uk/	Enables users to search for information relating to clinical and non-clinical evidence, and best practice across a broad spectrum of health and social care. Search parameters include a 'grey literature' option.
OpenGrey	a. General b. Online database	www.opengrey.eu/	Multidisciplinary European database which provides access to a range of grey literature, including technical and research reports, doctoral dissertations, conference papers and official publications. Covers a range of subject areas, including social science and humanities.
PsycINFO	a. Psychology and mental health b. Subscription database	Online but requires subscription (check if you have access with your institution or employer)	Provides access to abstracts and some full-text documents relating to the literature on psychology and mental health. Published by the American Psychological Association.
PubMed	a. Biomedicine & health b. Subscription database	Online but requires subscription (check if you have access with your institution or employer)	Very large database containing in excess of 21 million citations to biomedical and health-related literature. Some citations provide access to full-text documents.

Resource name	a. Subject area b. Type of resource	Web address	Brief guidance notes
Social Care Online	a. Social care b. Subject specialist portal	www.scie-socialcareonline.org.uk/	Contains a wide range of information on social work and social care, including grey literature such as circulars, good practice documents, policy documents, case studies, statistics and training materials.
Social Services Abstracts	a. Social work, human services and related b. Subscription database	Online but requires subscription (check if you have access with your institution or employer)	Provides access to abstracts and some full-text documents relating to research in social work and the human services, including social welfare, social policy and community development.
The Campbell Library (The Campbell Collaboration Library of Systematic Reviews)	a. Social welfare, education, crime and justice b. Online database/ library	www.campbellcollaboration. org/Library/Library.php	Provides access to a searchable library of systematic reviews focused on testing the effects of social interventions in the fields of education, social welfare and crime and justice.
The Cochrane Library	a. Health care b. Online database/ library	www.thecochranelibrary.com/	Comprises a collection of databases containing evidence-based material relating to health care decision making, including the Cochrane Database of Systematic Reviews. Cochrane Reviews are regarded as the 'gold standard' in respect of systematic reviews.
The King's Fund	a. Health & social care b. Website	www.kingsfund.org.uk/	Website for the King's Fund charity, which includes a substantial publications section covering health and social care topics. Many are available to freely download.
Web of Science	a. Science, technical, social sciences, arts and humanities b. Citation index	Online but requires subscription (check if you have access with your institution or employer)	Comprises a number of databases, including Social Sciences Citation Index (SSCI). Search options allow users to refine their search results using a number of criteria, including a 'social work' subject area category.
WorldCat	a. General b. Online library catalogue	www.worldcat.org/	Online 'mega-catalogue' which links to more than 10,000 libraries worldwide. Allows users to type in their postcode in order to find out where the closest libraries are which hold particular items. It would then be necessary to contact these libraries directly to enquire about reference access or borrowing.

Querying the database

Time suggested: 5–30 minutes (depending on what you already know!)

Attempt to answer all of the following questions. If you do not know the answers to any of these questions, then your task is to find out the answers.

1. What is the name of the search facility that your institution provides to help you search across all of the library's holdings? (If you are working in practice, what is the name of the main database for evidence-based research that you use to support your practice?)
2. What website address would you need to use to access this facility? (Can you access it at home or just on campus or at work?)
3. What kinds of materials does this service contain information about? Tick any of the following that apply:

      i.   Print journals   ☐
     ii.   Electronic journals   ☐
    iii.   Books   ☐
     iv.   Electronic books   ☐
      v.   Newspapers   ☐
     vi.   Book reviews   ☐
    vii.   Reference works   ☐
   viii.   Other   ☐

       (specify): ....

4. Does the service provided give you direct access to:

      i.   Abstracts of journal articles   ☐
     ii.   Full-text versions of journal articles   ☐
    iii.   Electronic books   ☐
     iv.   Other   ☐

       (specify): ....

Library catalogues

All libraries will have their own library catalogues (and in most cases these will exist as electronic catalogues). As well as showing you what's in stock and where to access items, they often allow users to place a 'hold' or 'reserve' facility on items that are currently out on loan. This is particularly handy as it means that you don't have to keep checking on the library catalogue or shelves to see if an item has been returned. Increasingly, library catalogues also contain links to electronic books which can often be accessed 'on the spot'.

How do you find grey literature?

As more and more material is made available online, it is becoming easier to access grey literature using **search engines** such as *Google* and *Google Scholar*

(Hartman, 2006). *Google Scholar* can be helpful in reducing the amount of irrelevant results that are returned as it aims to retrieve resources that are of scholarly or academic interest.

Social media tools, such as email lists, Twitter, blogs and discussion/bulletin boards, are also often a useful source of information, but like other forms of grey literature they are not subject to peer review and scrutiny in the same way that formally published material is. Many researchers use these tools as more informal ways of picking up leads and links to other sources of information.

CASE STUDY

SOCIALWORK-ALCOHOL-DRUGS @ JISCMail.ac.uk

Used with permission from www.jiscmail.ac.uk

SOCIALWORK-ALCOHOL-DRUGS is an email distribution list which exists for: 'social work academics, practitioners and students who have an interest in learning more about alcohol and drugs'.

To find this and other social work-related email lists, go to the JISCMail website at the following address and search the A–Z list: www.jiscmail.ac.uk/

You can browse or search the archives of most JISCMail lists, set up an account, and in many cases subscribe to lists yourself.

Other examples of useful social media websites include:

Blogs

Connecting Social Care and Social Media (http://shirleyayres.wordpress.com/). This blog, by a social care practitioner, explores the diverse ways in which social media can be used to enhance social care practice.

Social bookmarking

Delicious (www.delicious.com). This resource allows you to store and, more importantly, share your web links. A set of related links can be saved as a 'stack', and it is possible to search for stacks of links created by others on topics that you are interested in. One of the advantages of using a social bookmarking site is that it holds your links 'in the cloud' rather than saved to any particular computer, meaning you can access it from virtually any web-enabled device.

ACTIVITY

Student view of social media in social work

Time suggested: 20–30 minutes

Read the following newspaper article by Victoria Dixon (a second-year undergraduate social work student), who describes the ways in which she finds social media helpful to her studies. She also provides a set of links to interesting blogs and Twitter pages which provide a good introduction into the world of social media.

Dixon, V. (2011) 'Twitter is a great resource in social care', *The Guardian*, 12 December [Online]. Available at: www.guardian.co.uk/social-care-network/2011/dec/12/twitter-resource-social-care

If this link is no longer active, then search for it based on the title of the article.
　　Try accessing some of the links that Victoria Dixon mentions in her article.

Smarter searching

The secret to becoming a smarter searcher is to begin to explore and use the advanced search options that most databases, catalogues and some websites will provide. Not all advanced search options will work in the same way, so it's important to spend some time reading the 'help' pages that are built into most resources. Many advanced search options use 'Boolean operators' to help you to construct specific and sometimes complex search queries.

Boolean operators are special 'connecting' words that you can use to achieve specific kinds of results in your searches. Table 4.3 shows the three most common Boolean operator terms and the effect they have when included in your searches.

Table 4.3   Common Boolean operators

Boolean operator	What does it do?	Example
AND	Narrows your search	A search for child AND neglect will find only those sources that contain both the words 'child' and 'neglect'.
OR	Broadens your search	A search for child OR neglect will find sources which contain the word 'child' or sources which contain the word 'neglect' or sources which contain both words.
NOT	Searches for one term while excluding another	A search for child NOT neglect will only find sources which contain the word 'child' but not the word 'neglect'.

The Venn diagrams in Figure 4.1 provide a visual and accessible way of representing these searches.

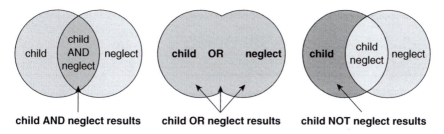

child AND neglect results   **child OR neglect results**   **child NOT neglect results**

Figure 4.1   Venn diagrams illustrating the use of common Boolean operators

Phrase searching can also be used in most databases (as well as search engines), and it is a way of searching for an exact phrase by putting quotation marks around it. So, if we searched for 'child neglect', only sources which used this exact phrase would be returned. However, if we searched for child neglect (without the quotation marks), sources would also be included which mention both of these words but not necessarily together in a phrase.

Social Services Abstracts

Selma is undertaking a literature review on recent examples of good practice in relation to child protection in the UK.

1. She begins by entering the following search terms into the 'Basic search' option:

(Continued)

(Continued)

Figure 4.2

This search returns 2567 results! But:

- Many results do not relate to the UK.
- Many results only mention child protection as a minor topic.
- Some results date from the mid-late twentieth century.

However, the results of this basic search have helped her to come to some conclusions about how she needs to narrow her search strategy.

2. Next she clicks on to the 'Advanced search' page and uses the search boxes and drop-down menu of Boolean operators to put together a more complex search:

Figure 4.3

- The first line begins with 'child protection OR child safeguard*' – notice how Selma is using the Boolean operator OR to combine different words which have very similar meanings, and using the truncation character to return variations of the word 'safeguard' (e.g. safeguard, safeguards, safeguarding).
- The second line begins with the Boolean operator AND, so this criterion will be added to the criterion in the first line, and contains different words to refer to young people (again, she has used the truncation character for the words child* and adolesc* to draw in other variations).
- The third line also begins with a Boolean AND, so this will be added to the previous two lines of criteria. This line contains variations of ways of referring to the United Kingdom (e.g. UK, Great Britain) as well as its constituent countries (England, Wales, Scotland and Northern Ireland).

Selma could have restricted the search to certain fields in the database, such as 'author name', 'title' or 'abstract', but instead she chooses to apply them to 'All fields' to begin with. She runs this 'Advanced search' and 1307 results are returned. This has obviously narrowed things down but there are still too many irrelevant results.

3. Selma applies some of the additional search criteria that Social Services Abstracts provides:

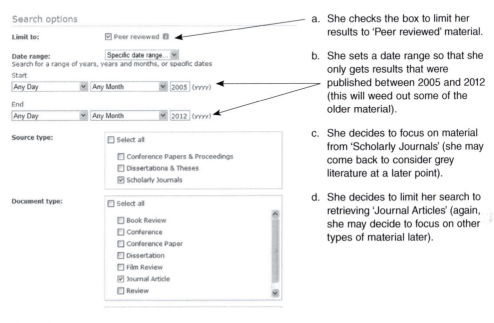

a. She checks the box to limit her results to 'Peer reviewed' material.

b. She sets a date range so that she only gets results that were published between 2005 and 2012 (this will weed out some of the older material).

c. She decides to focus on material from 'Scholarly Journals' (she may come back to consider grey literature at a later point).

d. She decides to limit her search to retrieving 'Journal Articles' (again, she may decide to focus on other types of material later).

Figure 4.4

She runs this search and 482 results are returned. The first few pages of these appear to be relevant to the subject of child protection, although closer reading of the abstracts will be necessary to identify which are the most useful.

4. Finally, in order to focus more specifically on 'good practice', Selma selects the option to 'Modify search' and adds another row to her 'Advanced search':

Figure 4.5

(Continued)

(Continued)

She uses the Boolean operator AND to add the criteria 'good practice OR best practice' to her search.

This new search returns 52 results, many of which look to be relevant and potentially useful.

Selma's literature searching emphasises some key points which we can apply to our own searching:

- Searching involves repeating and refining processes.
- Some techniques will broaden the search while others will narrow it.
- Advanced search options give you more control over your search.
- You learn more about what works and what doesn't as you progress through the search.
- You are looking for a balance between 'too much' and 'too little'.

ACTIVITY

Practise smarter searching

Time suggested: 20 minutes

1. Access the Social Care Online database, which is available at this web address: www.scie-socialcareonline.org.uk/
2. First use the 'Simple search' option to search for resources based on the topic of your literature review. Make some notes about how many results you retrieve and how useful these results are.
3. Next, click on the 'Intermediate search' option (this page offers similar options to the Social Services Abstracts 'Advanced search' page that we looked at previously). Try carrying out a number of searches using:

- different combinations of keywords
- different Boolean operators
- different fields (e.g. free text, topic, title, etc.).

Make some notes on the effectiveness of these searches.

NB: There is a link to a 'help with intermediate searching' page which may be useful to access if you are not clear about how intermediate searching works on this site.

3 Access and Evaluate

This stage is about accumulating material which appears to be useful and which you consider to be worth putting to one side for further consideration. The key to this process is to:

- be methodical and organised in terms of filing materials
- use the material you have found to help generate ideas for new potential sources.

Although you won't necessarily be reading the material you accumulate in detail at this stage, it's important to begin some kind of preliminary process of evaluation of what you find. This is so that you know whether you're on the rights lines and whether your search is progressing well or whether it would be helpful to modify your approach.

Be methodical and organised when filing materials

When carrying out a literature search, it can be very easy to find yourself becoming swamped in a sea of materials very quickly. So, decide on a method for filing your materials before you begin the search itself and stick to it. These filing systems can always be adapted and expanded as the search goes on.

There is no magic filing system which we would advocate here. The best approach is to adapt methods that you have used previously, are comfortable with and which feel manageable and realistic for you. However, Table 4.4 suggests some techniques which may be useful for both organising and conducting a preliminary evaluation of your materials.

Table 4.4   Tips for organising and evaluating materials

Method	How to do it
Traffic light colour coding, e.g.: **GREEN** – Very useful **AMBER** – Possibly useful **RED** – Not useful	After skim-reading your material, use coloured stickers (or different coloured folders) to make an initial assessment of how useful you feel it will be. By doing this you are prioritising what you need to focus on in more detail. Note that 'red' items are not discarded – it's useful to have a record of what was not useful, so that you don't go back and re-tread over old ground.
Numerical ordering system, e.g.: **1** – Very useful **2** – Possibly useful **3** – Not useful	This follows exactly the same principle as the colour-coding traffic light system, only in this case you are using a number-based ranking system. Simply write the appropriate number on each document at the top of the page. You might want to file each document into a corresponding '1', '2' or '3' folder.
Post-it note summaries	Note down your initial impressions of a document on a Post-it or sticky note and attach it to the first page of the document. Alternatively, use the 'Notes' section in software such as EndNote and Zotero to record your impressions.
Materials inventory	Develop an inventory or index of the materials that you accumulate so that you have a clear overview of what you've got. You can do this in a spreadsheet or word-processed document. Software like EndNote and Zotero allows you to store document information and documents themselves, and to run off lists of items. Use a colour-coding, numerical or other system to rank the usefulness of your materials.

Evaluating – moving forward with your search

As you access and accumulate more material, you are constantly building up your knowledge about:

- how much material is 'out there'
- what is useful and what is not

- what is readily available and what requires more time and effort to obtain
- which combinations of search techniques and search terms seem to yield the best results
- who the key authors and researchers are in your field.

This underlines the fact that the more immersed you are in the search process, the more productive and focused you become. Specific techniques, such as the 'snowball technique', can also be used to help you maximise your bank of useful materials.

The snowball technique

This is based on the idea that one useful source can provide additional leads to a number of other useful sources, and so on. You start 'small' and before you know it your search starts to 'snowball'. As it gets bigger and bigger, you accumulate more useful leads. The following activity demonstrates how this works.

ACTIVITY

Make your own snowball

Time suggested: 15–20 minutes

1. Find and access Jenny Pearce's 2011 article 'Working with trafficked children and young people: complexities in practice', *British Journal of Social Work*, vol. 41. If for any reason you cannot access this article, then choose one that is related to your own literature review topic or a topic you have studied previously.
2. Scan the abstract to get a general sense of what is discussed and then go to the reference list at the end of the article and count the number of references with titles which refer to the topic of child trafficking in the UK (or if you are choosing your own article/topic, count the number of references which directly relate to your topic).
3. Access one of these new sources, and again scan the reference list of this source to see how many relevant, new sources you can find.

Hopefully, what you will have found is that each article's reference list offers up a number of potentially promising sources that you can go on to track down and access. In Jenny Pearce's article there are 57 references in her reference list. A good number of these are directly related to the topic of child trafficking in the UK and would warrant further investigation. These include two references to items that the author has also written on the same topic, and these would therefore be well worth getting hold of.

4 Record and Review

The literature searching process is an important part of your methodology and it alerts the reader to how thorough and systematic you have been. Although you will hopefully be keeping notes and records as you carry out your search, as suggested in the previous sections, many people find it useful to develop this further into a diary or journal.

Literature review diaries and journals

A literature review diary or journal:

- is an ongoing record of your progress as you move through the different stages of your review process
- can be kept as a written hard-copy journal, a word-processed document or even online as a blog (consider whether public or private blogs are most appropriate)
- is an investment of your time, as many of the things that you record will be useful to you when it comes to writing up the final literature review.

Think about... Things to record in diaries/journals

For instance:

- Which keywords, and variations of these, did you identify and try out in your literature searching?
- Which online sources and databases did you use to search for materials? Did they provide many useful results?
- What ideas do you have for other resources that you might use to help with your search?
- How did you record the details of the sources that you've used so that you have these to hand when you come to cite and reference them in your literature review?
- Did you use any strategies, such as the four-stage approach outlined in this chapter or the 'snowball technique', in order to expand your range of useful resources?
- What worked well and what was less successful?

Challenges and How to Overcome Them

Despite our best efforts, there will always be occasions when we feel our literature searching is not as productive as we would like it to be. Table 4.5 lists some of the most common challenges and suggests some practical strategies for helping to overcome these.

Table 4.5   Challenges in searching the literature and some strategies to overcome them

Challenge	Strategies
Being unsure of where to even begin!	• Use your topic area or title (if you have one) to help you to identify search criteria and relevant keywords
Being unable to find enough information	• Try alternative keywords • Use the Boolean operator OR to broaden your results • Consider altering the focus of your topic if not much has been published on your chosen area

(Continued)

Table 4.5   (Continued)

Challenge	Strategies
	• Use a range of catalogues, databases and search engines • Ask colleagues for leads • Try the snowball technique
Finding lots of irrelevant results	• Use the Boolean operator NOT to exclude irrelevant topics • Use more specific keywords to make your results more focused – e.g. use UK, United Kingdom, etc., if you wish to focus on that geographical area • Switch from general search engines to more specific search tools and subject-related websites
Getting too bogged down in trying to read and understand the first few things that you find	• Put things to one side and carry on with your search – the time to read in detail and digest will come later!
Feeling swamped with too much information	• Use smart reading techniques like skim-reading abstracts, introductions and conclusions and discard anything that doesn't sound relevant. (For more on reading techniques, see Chapter 5) • Rank or colour code the relevance of resources you find
Keeping track of lots of documents	• Get into the habit of using a filing system early on – it doesn't matter which one, as long as you are consistent • Print off journal articles or keep electronic copies • Take down details of sources in order to allow you to find them again and produce appropriate references
Losing focus and drifting off-topic	• Remind yourself of your title (if you have one) or your topic keywords • Put material which is 'interesting' but not relevant to one side • Be realistic about how much you can cover in your literature review. Linked themes and sub-topics are almost endless, but your job is to stay on topic
Losing motivation	• Searching can be exciting at times, but it can also be tedious, tiring and mentally demanding – take regular breaks • Try to diagnose your motivation issue(s). Then use the strategies offered here to help you move forward

Ideas for Taking Things Further

1. Using the methods and resources discussed in this chapter, search for an example of a literature review related to social care. You do not need to read the entire document, but instead read the methodology section which addresses how the literature search was carried out. Which techniques and processes were used?
2. Read the 'Summary' and 'Discussion' sections of Clapton's (2010) *SCIE Report 34: Bibliographic Databases for Social Care Searching* (see reference list below

for full details and web address). This report compares the coverage of different databases and explains why social care can be a challenging field to search.

3. Cultivate good searching habits by challenging yourself to always use the advanced search options whenever you search a catalogue, database or search engine. Try to maintain it for at least a week!

Chapter Summary

- We have outlined a four-stage process of conducting a literature review: (1) identifying search criteria, (2) searching resources, (3) accessing and evaluating resources, and (4) recording and reviewing the search process.
- We have introduced a range of useful resources which can be used to find materials, including general and specialised databases, library catalogues and web resources.
- We have considered the advantages of using advanced search options for your literature searching.
- We have suggested strategies for dealing with some of the common problems that can arise when conducting a literature search.

Further Reading and Useful Resources

Aveyard, H. (2007) *Doing a Literature Review in Health and Social Care*. Maidenhead: Open University Press. (Chapter 4 focuses on the process of searching for relevant literature.)

Dolowitz, D., Buckler, S. and Sweeney, F. (2008) *Researching Online*. Basingstoke: Palgrave Macmillan. (This book will help you to get to grips with some of the varied online resources that can be used in academic research. It is not specifically focused on social work, but its general points and guidance can be applied to carrying out your literature review.)

Munger, D. and Campbell, S. (2012) *What Every Student Needs to Know About Researching Online*. New York: Pearson/Longman. (Contains some useful chapters on evaluating your sources and finding the right information, and also discusses how social media tools can be used for research.)

Ridley, D. (2008) *The Literature Review: A Step-by-Step Guide for Students*. London: Sage. (Chapter 3, 'Sources of information and conducting searches', provides some helpful suggestions of tools and techniques for information searching.)

Rumsey, S. (2008) *How to Find Information* (2nd edition). Maidenhead: Open University Press. (This text covers all aspects of finding information – from the planning stage to carrying out, evaluating, recording and managing searches.)

Stogdon, C. and Kiteley, R. (2010) *Study Skills for Social Workers*. Sage Study Skills Series. London: Sage. (Chapter 6, 'Researching, reading and critiquing', includes guidance on a multi-step search strategy and the 'snowball technique' discussed in this chapter.)

References

Alcock, P., Erskine, A. and May, M. (2002) *The Blackwell Dictionary of Social Policy*. Oxford: Blackwell.

Clapton, J. (2010) *SCIE Report 34: Bibliographic Databases for Social Care Searching* [Online]. London: Social Care Institute for Excellence (SCIE). Available at: www.scie.org. uk/publications/reports/report34.pdf (accessed 5 January 2012).

Grayson, L. and Gomersall, A. (2003) *A Difficult Business: Finding the Evidence for Social Science Reviews*. ESRC UK Centre for Evidence Based Policy and Practice Working Paper 19. Available at: www.kcl.ac.uk/sspp/departments/politicaleconomy/research/cep/pubs/papers/assets/wp19.pdf (accessed 18 November 2006).

Hartman, K.A. (2006) 'Social policy resources for social work: grey literature and the internet', *Behavioural & Social Sciences Librarian*, 25(1): 1–11.

Holden, G., Barker, K., Covert-Vail, L., Rosenberg, G. and Cohen, S.A. (2008) 'Does Social Work Abstracts work?', *Research on Social Work Practice*, 18(5): 487–499.

Pearce, J.J. (2011) 'Working with trafficked children and young people: complexities in practice', *British Journal of Social Work*, 41: 1424–1441.

Pierson, J. and Thomas, M. (2010) *Dictionary of Social Work*. Maidenhead: Open University Press.

5

Reading with a Purpose

☑ **Learning Outcomes** ☑

- To develop an understanding of academic reading as an active process
- To be able to apply different approaches to reading material, including quick-overview reading, 'getting the gist' reading and critical/analytical reading
- To learn about a range of practical strategies that can help you to manage the specific challenges involved in reading for literature reviews
- To develop an awareness of reading tools, such as PQRST

We have separated the processes of reading, critical and analytical thinking, note-taking and writing over the next four chapters in order to emphasise their particular issues and challenges. However, it's important to realise that in practice these things are closely intertwined. It would be most useful for you to read these four chapters together as this will reinforce your awareness of the ways in which each supports the others.

Reading for Literature Reviews

> Avoid an educational process that only provides you with information; rather your brain needs training in how to use information, how to think creatively from that information, how to critique. (Metcalfe, 2006: 3)

To a great extent, the success of your literature review rests on finding enough relevant literature on your chosen topic and, most importantly, demonstrating that you have read, digested and thought about the issues and implications raised by the literature. The effort and hard work that you have put into your literature searching, as we discussed in the previous chapter, will pay dividends when it comes to the reading stage. While any type of reading for academic purposes will involve a similar set of challenges, we suggest that they are often intensified when reading for literature review purposes. Table 5.1 lists some of the challenges and requirements of reading for your literature review.

Table 5.1   The challenges and requirements of reading for literature reviews

Challenges	Requirements
Volume of reading required	• Literature reviews call for a broad range of relevant reading • Requires sifting through many sources • Requires a level of resilience as it can be physically and mentally tiring
Managing reading time	• Requires effective time-management skills • Will be challenging as you learn to balance this with other commitments, such as work, study or family/friends
Maintaining focus	• Requires an ability to remain focused on your topic, while also considering the potential relevance of things you may not have considered • Requires a clear goal and an ethos of purposeful reading
Selecting and prioritising	• Requires the ability to discern what is most useful and potentially relevant, which in itself draws on an ability to make a pre-assessment of the reading material • Requires an ability to establish an order of priority in terms of which reading should be tackled first. This may be reassessed as the reading process progresses
Summarising and condensing masses of information	• Requires not only that you comprehend a text, but that you can extract what is most useful/relevant about it and put it into your own précis/summary • Requires judgement in weeding out things which are less relevant to your topic and/or approach
Sustaining critical analysis	• Requires sustaining an enquiring, critical and interactive approach to reading which can be mentally taxing • Requires an effort to resist 'automatic pilot' reading
Keeping track of notes, ideas, themes, concepts	• Academic reading involves an input < > output process – you need to both absorb and respond to the material, and keep track of your thoughts and ideas • Requires effective thinking and note-taking skills
Encountering the 'unfamiliar'	• New subjects and topics bring new ideas, concepts and vocabulary – this can be both stimulating and disorientating • Requires an ability to accept, or at least be comfortable with, some degree of uncertainty • Losing one's familiar bearings is usually a fundamental part of the learning process

Your personal reading profile

Time suggested: 15 minutes

It's useful to approach the substantial task of reading for a literature review with a clear idea of the kinds of challenges that this will pose for you.

- Based on your previous reading experiences, make a list of these likely challenges.
- As you read through the rest of this chapter, note down any possible strategies, techniques or ideas that you could use to help you to manage or successfully overcome these challenges.

Ways of Reading

Passive reading

Casual reading (e.g. reading novels, magazines, general internet browsing) is often characterised by a 'passive mode', where we allow ourselves to be carried along by the story or the drama of the piece. Often, we want to be stimulated and entertained, or we may simply be browsing for information. While there is nothing wrong with casual reading (and it certainly has its place in many people's repertoire of leisure activities), difficulties arise if we take the same kind of largely passive approach to academic reading.

Active reading

Academic reading requires a more active process in order to be useful and productive. Your aim is not simply to report on, or even summarise, what you read, but to think about it, and reflect on it, in an informed and critical manner. Consider the act of reading as being more of a dialogue or exchange between you and the author, instead of a one-way, passive process. Table 5.2 provides some strategies for active reading.

Table 5.2   Active reading – ask for more from the text!

Strategy	Example
Question what you think the author is stating	'Although this author seems to be supporting the idea of learning journals as an aid to social work education, is he in fact suggesting that they are only really useful in certain contexts, and not in others?'

(Continued)

Table 5.2   (Continued)

Strategy	Example
Identify how the writing is structured and think about how this can be used to convey thoughts and ideas	'The first part of the report **describes** the historical background around Risk Factor Analysis (RFA). The second section **explains** how current practice has been shaped by RFA. The third section **demonstrates** limitations of RFA. The final section **proposes** a novel holistic approach in response to limitations addressed in the previous section.' *In this example the author moves from describing and explaining to demonstrating limitations and finally proposing something new.*
Consider the implications of the language and terminology that has been used	'What does it mean to describe a social worker as being "culturally competent"? When (and why) did this term gain currency and what are the implications of its use? Does it carry any political and ideological connotations? Is the use of this term consistent across the literature or is it a problematic or contested term?'
Identify terms, expressions or phrases which are unfamiliar to you and consider how you could gain clarity in relation to these	'This literature review mentions "life review therapy" several times but I've never heard of it. Maybe I could find a definition in a social work, psychology or counselling dictionary, or using a reputable online glossary of terms?'
Be prepared to ask challenging questions: How, what, who, when, where, why?	'**How** did the research team ensure that no bias entered the data analysis stage?'
	'**What** are reasons why this intervention was found to be ineffective, in some practice contexts?'
	'**Who** is not being heard or represented in this account?'
	'**When** was this research first carried out and what impact did the social, historical, economic or political context of that time have on the approach taken?'
	'**Where** (in which environment) was the research carried out?'
	'**Why** were some search terms used in this literature search, but not other more obvious ones?'
Become a detective – always be on the look-out for valid and reliable evidence, and question what is presented as evidence	'There is only one key source used to support the author's main argument. That source is from research carried out in the 1970s in a completely different practice context.'
Separate the wheat from the chaff. Not everything that you read is going to be useful, interesting, well written or even particularly insightful	'This paper is not very well written and it doesn't really seem to add anything that has not already been stated in the literature. However, there is one useful note about limitations of qualitative analysis, and I will refer to this in my literature review.'

Recognising 'signal' words

Active reading involves being aware of the ways in which language can be used to have a particular effect on the reader. One aspect of this is learning to recognise signal words that can help you to understand where the author is heading (the route or path they are taking), and what they are attempting to achieve. Remember that these signal words will have been carefully chosen to support and emphasise the author's points. So, don't be afraid to look 'behind' words and critically reflect on the persuasive power of language (known as 'rhetoric'). Table 5.3 provides some examples of the types of common signal words found in academic writing (adapted from Langan, 2002: 391–396), but you will no doubt think of others.

Table 5.3 Signal words and how they are used

Type of signal word	Examples of signal words/phrases
Emphasis (signals that particular significance is being given to something – helps to focus the reader's attention)	...a **primary** concern / ...a **key** feature / ...a **central** issue / ....a **major** factor, etc.
Addition (signals that a number of related points are being proposed – often used to lend weight to a particular perspective)	...in **addition** / ...**also** / ...**secondly** /...and **finally**, etc.
Comparison/Contrast (signals that one or more things are being weighed up or evaluated in relation to other things – helps to establish the relative merits of different things)	...**likewise** / ...in the **same way**... / ...**similarly** / ...in a **different way**, etc.
Illustration (signals that the writer is showing how something works or operates – useful for demonstrating connections between theory and practice)	...**for example** / ...**for instance** / ...**such as**, etc.
Cause and effect (signals that the writer is suggesting that a particular event leads to particular consequences – useful for constructing a logical sequence in an argument)	...as a **result of**... / ...**therefore**... / ...**because** / ...**results in**..., etc.

Developing your vocabulary

One of the things that you will be doing throughout your academic reading is extending and refining your vocabulary. You should be aiming to nurture an accurate and nuanced understanding of the language or 'jargon' that is used within the field of social work practice and research.

Defining terms

Time suggested: 20–30 minutes

Spend a few minutes writing a brief definition for each of these terms based on your current understanding of them:

(Continued)

ACTIVITY

(Continued)

- accountability
- anti-discriminatory practice
- consent to share information
- evidence base
- person-centred approach
- social exclusion.

Now look for some formal definitions of these terms, using a specialist social work dictionary, a glossary in a social work textbook or a reputable online glossary.
    Compare your own definitions of the terms with the formal definitions you have found:

- How complete were your own definitions?
- Were there any important aspects of these terms which you missed out?

This exercise highlights that even when we understand certain terms we may not always be able to offer a full or specialist definition of them.

Practical tips for engaging with texts

Active reading requires us to acknowledge and record our responses to what we read, whether those responses are in the form of thoughts, feelings, ideas or questions. There are various practical methods you can use to help with this, such as:

- writing notes and ideas on Post-it notes and sticking these to the relevant page or paragraph (always remember to remove these if you are borrowing an item)
- photocopying/printing book chapters, journal articles or reports so that you can fully annotate your own personal copy
- using the highlighter, bookmarking and comments tools in software such as Adobe Reader, word-processing software and E-book readers
- using online note-making services when reading online, such as the free service 'Evernote' (www.evernote.com). These services typically allow you to save notes, images, voice-notes, online videos and copies of web pages to the 'cloud', so that they can be accessed wherever you have a web connection.

Pre-reading

'Pre-reading' describes the activity that we do before getting into detailed reading of a text. It is a useful stage as it helps us to orient ourselves in relation to what we are going to read.

Textmapping

'Textmapping' is a visual approach to pre-reading which involves marking up texts in order to see how they are structured and how their different components fit together to form a complete whole. Advocates suggest that this visual approach to pre-reading assists with effective comprehension (Middlebrook, n.d.). Table 5.4 offers a quick guide to textmapping.

Table 5.4   A quick guide to textmapping

Step	How to do this
1 Create a 'scroll'	Print out a copy of your article, book chapter or web document (textmapping works best with short documents as opposed to complete books). Arrange the document in page order, one page next to the other, in a long line going from left to right and use adhesive tape to stick these together to form a long scroll (see example below).

2 Map (mark up) scroll	Use coloured pens or highlighters to mark up different sections of your text. For example:

1   Highlight the main title (red)
2   Highlight all of the sub-titles (blue)
3   Highlight any keywords (purple)
4   Draw a box around the abstract (green)
5   Draw a box around the introduction (orange)
6   Draw a box around the conclusion (pink)
7   Highlight diagrams, tables, charts or illustrations (yellow)
8   Draw a box around the references section (brown)
9   Highlight new terminology and/or definitions of terms, and so on. Some documents will contain alternative/different features to mark up

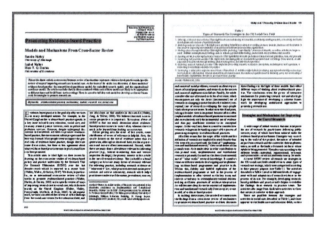

Sample pages from a mapped text

3 Observe	Look over the mapped document and note how the document is presented, organised and structured. How much weight of text is given to each section? How do sections fit together in order to create a sense of logical flow?

We are not suggesting that you will have the time or inclination to do this with every text you read, but it is worth doing it with at least one journal article and book chapter to help you to consciously focus on the pre-reading stage, and the useful knowledge that can be gained from this.

Reading for Different Purposes

This section identifies three different types of reading that it can be useful to adopt at different stages of your literature review reading:

1. Quick overview reading (see Table 5.5)
2. 'Getting the gist' reading (see Table 5.6)
3. Critical and analytical reading (see Table 5.7)

Table 5.5   Quick overview reading

1. Quick overview reading	
What is it?	• Used to gain a quick insight into whether a particular source is likely to be useful or not • Helps to identify parts or sections of sources which may be particularly relevant • Usually takes the form of scanning or skim-reading • Can be done quite quickly • No need to get bogged down with detail at this point
When is it used?	• In early to mid stages of reading process • Can overlap with literature searching process • Useful for sifting through a large quantity of material
How is it done?	Use the text's own navigational tools: • **Read the contents page** – it's designed to show you what is covered and how to get there (e.g. page numbers) • **Scan indexes** – not all publications have indexes but most academic books will have them. Glance through them to see if any of your search terms (or similar phrases) appear and how thorough the coverage is (e.g. one page? several pages?) • **Read introductions** to get a quick overview of an individual book chapter, journal article or report • **Read chapter conclusions, abstracts, summaries** as these should all summarise the key issues covered

ACTIVITY

Find it fast! Practise quick overview reading

Time suggested: 30 minutes

Using the topic of your literature review (or a topic of your choosing), identify some relevant texts and spend some time using the quick overview reading techniques.

- Aim to spend no more than 3–5 minutes getting a quick overview of each text, and try to evaluate the usefulness of at least six sources.
- It might be helpful to do this in a library where you can access several different texts or use an online database or search engine (see Chapter 4 for ideas).

Table 5.6   'Getting the gist' reading

2. 'Getting the gist' reading	
What is it?	• Reading that gives you a basic familiarity with the content of the text, e.g. what it is discussing and what the main points are • Usually required in situations when you are fairly unfamiliar with a text
When is it done?	• Once you've carried out your quick overview reading • When focusing on texts which seem relevant to your literature review topic • When re-acquainting yourself with something that you've already read in the past
How is it done?	• Identify the question(s) the text is attempting to address • List the key points the author is making (the norm is one key point per paragraph although this is not always the case). Try to summarise each paragraph in a brief sentence • Notice what kinds of evidence are used to support points and the extent to which evidence is used • Try to get a feel for the structure of the text and how this may help to support the main arguments being made • Aim to identify what the main findings or conclusions are • Highlight or make a note of anything you don't understand or which isn't clear

Getting the gist

ACTIVITY

Time suggested: 20–30 minutes

Take one of the sources you used in the previous 'Find it fast!' activity and apply the process of 'getting the gist' reading outlined above. Use a print-out or photocopy of your source so that you can mark and annotate the text.

Table 5.7   Critical and analytical reading

3. Critical and analytical reading	
What is it?	• Involved, in-depth reading which requires closer attention to detail (often slower and more time-consuming) • Reading which poses searching and probing questions of the text
When is it done?	• After 'getting the gist' reading (NB: Even if you know from the outset that certain texts are going to be essential to your literature review, it is still useful to use 'getting the gist' reading first to gain a basic familiarity with them)

(Continued)

Table 5.7   (Continued)

3. Critical and analytical reading

How is it done?	• By avoiding taking things at 'face value', but instead asking questions of, or 'interrogating', the text
	• By evaluating the credibility and appropriateness of the evidence presented and the arguments constructed:
	o Is evidence 'reliable' or 'valid'?
	o What are the strengths and limitations of the evidence?
	• By using skills of critical analysis to weigh up the strengths/flaws in the points that have been made:
	o Are points clear or confused?
	o Has the author acknowledged areas of weakness in their argument(s) in addition to the strengths claimed?
	• By critically examining each stage of the research/investigation process for evidence that it has been carried out in an appropriate way
	• By looking for evidence of steps taken to make the research process transparent, and the efforts made to avoid bias in data collection, data analysis and formulation of conclusions
	• By examining whether points are factually correct/accurate
	• By considering the political implications of what has been suggested
	• By identifying gaps, omissions or oversights in the material covered
	• By being aware of what your 'gut feelings' are about the piece:
	o Does it inspire confidence in you? Does it irritate you? Does it feel as if something is not quite right?
	o Intuitive feelings and responses can be useful initial starting points, but they need to be followed up and substantiated with reasoning which is supported by evidence
	• By considering whether the piece raises any ethical issues or considerations:
	o Have these been acknowledged and addressed in the text?
	• By considering how future practice and/or research could be extended, developed or changed as a result of this work

Critical and analytical reading

ACTIVITY

Time suggested: 30–45 minutes

Read through the following introduction to a literature review. Use your critical and analytical reading skills (and Table 5.7) to help you to highlight any problems, issues or questions that arise. We have numbered each sentence in order to help you link your comments to particular sentences. (Refer to the end of this chapter for our thoughts in response to this exercise.)

Social work and evidence-based practice

There is widespread agreement that evidence-based practice is the key to improving social work practice (1). This is supported by the fact that it is already used in areas such as health care, education and several others (2). Research in these areas has proven that evidence-based practice leads to better informed decision making by practitioners, and this will naturally lead to better outcomes for service users (3). There are many different competing definitions of evidence-based practice but, for the sake of clarity, this literature review will simply define it as 'the requirement to use research evidence in order to guide decision making and action in practice' (4). Most social work courses, these days, will promote the use of evidence-based approaches (5). However, the research from a case study of evidence-based social work practice, carried out in a London borough in 2001 (Dwyer, 2002), indicated that 'on the ground' the adoption of it is piecemeal and inconsistent (6). Some people would argue that evidence-based approaches encourage social workers to be less responsive to the particular needs of individual clients (7). However, others counter this argument by highlighting the serious failures of the care system in recent years, as reported in the mainstream media, and argue that evidence-based approaches can assist practitioners in making more effective assessments and decisions (8). Although there are arguments on both sides, it seems obvious that social work requires a high degree of sensitivity to what is going on in a particular case, and that 'gut feelings' and intuition are just as important in decision-making processes as academic research (9).

Reading Tools

Some people prefer to use more structured approaches to get the most out of their academic reading and you may already have come across reading tools such as the SQ3R approach (Robinson, 1970), which we discuss in Chapter 6 of *Study Skills for Social Workers* (Stogdon and Kiteley, 2010). There are many different variations of these tools, which tend to incorporate the 'quick overview', 'getting the gist' and 'critical and analytical' types of reading we have just discussed.

Most reading tools share the same basic aims of:

- encouraging you to be clearer about the reasons why you are reading
- focusing your attention on the material which is potentially most useful to you
- prompting you to be questioning and enquiring while you read
- encouraging you to review and test your understanding of the material that you've read, which in turn leads to improved learning and recall
- providing a systematic approach to reading which jolts you out of any passive, unfocused or unquestioning reading approaches that you may have slipped into.

We have chosen to include the PQRST reading tool in this chapter. The name is an acronym that derives from the first letter of each of the steps involved, as shown in Table 5.8.

We have repeatedly stressed the value of asking questions of the text, and this is a key step in the PQRST approach detailed below. A helpful tip for doing this is included in the following 'Did you know?' box.

Table 5.8   The PQRST reading tool

Step	Achieved by	Purpose
Preview	Skim-read, paying particular attention to titles, sub-titles, abstracts, introductions, conclusions, summaries in order to get a basic grasp of the text. Alternatively, use the textmapping approach described earlier in this chapter.	Provides you with an overview and mental map of the text
Question	Identify the questions that you need the text to answer or address, as well as any questions that have arisen from your preview reading. The 'turning statements into questions' approach can help with this (see below).	Encourages you to think about why you are reading and what you want to get out of it, providing focus and direction
Read	Read the text in detail and use the knowledge you have gained from the preview, and questions identified in the previous step, to help you to stay focused. Also, refer back to the 'how is it done?' section of Table 5.7 (Critical and analytical reading).	Previous stages prepare you to read actively and with a view to meeting your identified learning needs
Summarise	Aim to summarise the key points that the text has put forward *in your own words*. You can use lists, diagrams, charts or any other methods that you find useful. Aim to get down major points rather than irrelevant detail. Refer to Chapter 7 for more on effective note-taking.	Translates the reading into a form which makes sense to you, encouraging you to make links with things that are already familiar
Test	Go back to the questions you raised in the second step and attempt to answer these based on what you have learnt from your reading. Try to define important concepts and recall key points. Practise this skill to help you strengthen your ability to focus while reading, and to recall important information afterwards.	Tests your levels of comprehension and highlights areas which you may need to spend more time on or which require re-reading

?   Did you know? Turning statements into questions   ?

How might the heading 'Alcohol, drug use and domestic violence' be turned into a useful question?
  Some of our suggestions include:

  What is the relationship (if any) between alcohol, drug use and incidences of domestic violence?

Or:

> What evidence is there to suggest a relationship between alcohol use, drug use and domestic violence?

Or:

> How might alcohol and drug use impact on the lives of the perpetrators and victims of domestic violence?

Reading about Literature Reviewing

Most of your reading should focus directly on the body of literature relating to the topic of your review. We might describe this as reading *for* the purposes of literature reviewing. However, there is a secondary area of reading that you should be engaging in and we can refer to this as reading *about* literature reviewing. This will be 'stuff' relating to many of the topics addressed in this book, including methods, methodology, theoretical approaches, critical frameworks, and wider debates relating to the question of knowledge production in social work practice. Reasons for reading *about* literature reviewing include:

- It can usefully inform your own literature review process.
- It allows you to speak with more insight and confidence about the many choices you have made during every stage of your literature review.
- It enables you to demonstrate an informed perspective around questions of methods and methodology, including a critical appraisal of their respective strengths and weaknesses, as reported in the wider literature.
- It demonstrates that you are engaging with current issues in the way that social work practice is investigated.

When searching for this type of literature, use search terms that clearly relate to the processes involved in undertaking literature reviews. Some academic journals focus on particular research approaches and methodologies (e.g. *Qualitative Social Work*) and/or theoretical positions (e.g. *Feminist Review*). Also, websites such as that of the Social Care Institute for Excellence (SCIE) (www.scie.org.uk/) have many resources which critically discuss the process of conducting literature and knowledge reviews.

Reading tactics – quick tips for successful reading

In tutorials, students often indicate that doing enough quality reading is one of the areas they most struggle with. We conclude this chapter with some of the basic tactics that can be used to make the process less painful and more rewarding (see Table 5.9).

Table 5.9   Tactics and tips for successful reading

Tactic	Can be achieved by
Chunk your reading time **Aims:** • To prevent overload and burn-out • To delay onset of boredom or distraction • To defuse frustration	✓ Reading for short, regular intervals of time, e.g. 20-minute blocks ✓ Having short breaks between blocks of reading time ✓ Stretching, getting up and walking about and breathing exercises can all help to re-energise you and prevent you becoming lethargic ✓ Identifying short blocks of time during the day that might not otherwise be used for anything in particular ✓ Knowing when you need to stop – there's no point reading if you're not taking anything in
Make meaningful notes **Aims:** • To ensure reading is productive • To encourage active reading • To provide valuable material for you to develop in your writing	✓ Reminding yourself of the questions you are seeking to address and focusing your note-taking on these issues ✓ Avoiding copying large sections of text word for word – this can feel very productive but is actually very passive ✓ Using notes to record your own responses to what you are reading about as well as the details of what you are reading
Turn problems or difficulties into tasks and challenges **Aims:** • To keep you actively engaged • To avoid becoming lost or disheartened • To extend your knowledge and understanding	✓ Getting into the habit of looking up the definition of unfamiliar words/terms ✓ Looking for alternative explanations of concepts or ideas, if you are unsure about anything you read ✓ Generating 'to do' lists, when confronted with things you don't understand or find especially difficult, in which you list possible ways of overcoming these difficulties
Re-read **Aims:** • To develop your understanding of the material • To give yourself more opportunity to digest difficult material • To promote greater familiarity with the 'discourse' of your topic area	✓ Trying to find enough time to re-read material. Some academic texts are so detailed and dense with information that they are practically impossible to absorb and process on one reading alone ✓ Being strategic in your re-reading – perhaps some sections are more crucial than others? ✓ After you have read and made notes on a text, trying to re-read (skim) parts to make sure you haven't missed out any crucial things

Ideas for Taking Things Further

1. Select an academic article or book chapter that relates to the topic of your literature review, then use the text's headings or selected statements to help generate a set of at least five questions to make your reading more focused and enquiring.
2. Take a second article or short book chapter and:

   i. Use the textmapping technique to create a scroll and map the text using highlighter pens.
   ii. Highlight any signal words and make a note of what type of signal word they are (e.g. emphasis, addition, comparison, etc.).
   iii. Read the text using the PQRST technique and, as you do so, annotate the text with your questions, comments, remarks and thoughts.

3. Read something that you find particularly challenging (in terms of intellectual content as opposed to subject matter) and list any difficulties that you encounter. Next, apply your problem-solving skills to identify any strategies that you could use to help you with these. Try to ensure that any strategies that you identify are SMART (<u>S</u>pecific, <u>M</u>easurable, <u>A</u>chievable, <u>R</u>elevant, <u>T</u>ime delimited) in order to gain maximum benefit from them.

Critical and analytical reading

General – Clearly the problems with this piece have been exaggerated for the purposes of the exercise, but in general we can identify that it has poor logical flow and statements often seem abrupt and disjointed and are rarely supported by evidence.

Sentence 1 – If there is widespread agreement about the role of evidence-based practice, why has the writer not supplied some citations to sources which confirm or corroborate this? How can we evaluate this evidence for ourselves if we don't know where to find it?

Sentence 2 – The writer has listed some specific contexts (e.g. heath care, education) but has not provided any examples or illustrations. The phrase 'several others' is vague and suggests that the writer is not fully aware of the context.

Sentence 3 – The writer has inferred that better outcomes for service users will result from practitioners' evidence-based decision making, but has not developed a case to say why this is necessarily so. For instance, how is 'better informed decision making' even identified and assessed?

Sentence 4 – The writer is correct to seek to define key terms, but the problem here is that we don't know where this definition has been taken from, so we cannot judge if it is likely to be a reliable source or not. Also, if there are many competing definitions, then some investigation and comparison of these would have lead to a more sophisticated and nuanced understanding of the term.

Sentence 5 – While this may be true, the statement is generalised. Briefly tracing the emergence of evidence-based practice in social work education may have provided more useful information and context.

Sentence 6 – While the cited study provides some useful evidence, to what extent can we extrapolate wider assumptions about the field of social work practice based on a single

COMMENTS ON ACTIVITY

(Continued)

(Continued)

study in one London borough? What would we need to know in order to judge whether this one case may be 'typical' or 'representative' of others?

Sentence 7 – Who are these 'some people'? The writer needs to find this view expressed in a published document or artefact and cite and reference this in their work, so that 'some people' becomes a list of identifiable, named authors/commentators.

Sentence 8 – Again, who are these 'others'? Also, the statement about high-profile media cases needs to be much more specific by clearly referring to particular cases, and needs to explain how such cases might raise arguments in favour of evidence-based practice.

Sentence 9 – The writer casually rounds off their discussion with a contentious and controversial statement, but does not provide any evidence or logical argument to support this point.

Chapter Summary

- We have considered ways in which 'academic reading' requires a more active approach than casual or everyday reading.
- We have considered the specific challenges involved in reading for literature reviews, and have explored practical strategies that can assist in this process.
- We have considered three different types of reading (1. Quick overview, 2. Getting the gist, 3. Critical and analytical), which each have specific uses at different stages in the reading process.
- We have explained the use of a particular reading strategy known as PQRST, which is designed to help you get more out of your academic reading.

Further Reading and Useful Resources

Cottrell, S. (2011) *Critical Thinking Skills: Developing Effective Analysis and Argument* (2nd edition). Basingstoke: Palgrave Macmillan. (See especially Chapter 9, 'Critical reading and note-making: Critical selection, interpretation and noting of source material'.)

Fairbairn, G. and Fairbairn, S. (2001) *Reading at University*. Buckingham: Open University Press. (This book provides a good introduction to what characterises reading for academic work, but note that it is not focused on any one particular academic discipline.)

Hart, C. (1998) *Doing a Literature Review*. London: Sage. (See especially Chapter 3, 'Classifying and reading research'.)

Metcalfe, M. (2006) *Reading Critically at University*. London: Sage. (This book provides a thorough appraisal of tools and techniques that can be used when critiquing the material that you read, and it is recommended for readers who like to think deeply about different ways of thinking.)

Ridley, D. (2008) *The Literature Review: A Step-by-Step Guide*. London: Sage. (See Chapter 4, 'Reading and note taking strategies'.)

Stogdon, C. and Kiteley, R. (2010) *Study Skills for Social Workers*. Sage Study Skills Series. London: Sage. (See Chapter 6, 'Researching, reading and critiquing'.)

Wallace, M. and Wray, A. (2006) *Critical Reading and Writing for Postgraduate Students*. London: Sage. (Although this book is written specifically for postgraduate students, it will be of use to any reader who wants to develop their critical reading and writing skills. It also directly addresses issues to do with the process of producing a literature review.)

References

Langan, J. (2002) *Reading and Study Skills* (2nd edition). New York: McGraw-Hill.

Metcalfe, M. (2006) *Reading Critically at University*. London: Sage.

Middlebrook, D. (n.d.) *The Textmapping Project* [Online]. Available at: www.textmapping. org/index.html (accessed 15 August 2012).

Robinson, F.P. (1970) *Effective Study* (4th edition). New York: Harper & Row.

Stogdon, C. and Kiteley, R. (2010) *Study Skills for Social Workers*. Sage Study Skills Series. London: Sage.

6

Developing Your Critical and Analytical Skills

☑ **Learning Outcomes** ☑

- To understand the significance and perspective of the author(s) of the literature that you are reviewing and also to consider when, where and why it was written
- To develop confidence in identifying any potential bias in the writing and to assess the academic credibility of the literature that is being considered
- To contextualise the literature in the context of received wisdom on the topic and current thinking, alongside consideration of any dissenting voices and alternative perspectives that may be relevant
- To develop and apply your repertoire of professional social work skills of critical thinking and analysis to the academic context of your literature review

? Did you know? Defining the purpose of a literature review ?

This is how Jesson et al. (2011: 10) define the purpose of a literature review:

> Where you will show that you are both aware of and can interpret what is already known and where eventually you will be able to point out the contradictions and gaps in existing knowledge.

Who, When, Where and Why?

Posing these questions will help you to develop the skills that you will require to critically analyse the selected literature for your review.

In Chapter 3 we looked briefly at an example topic for literature review study in relation to young black British men who are over-represented in restrictive mental health services in the UK, and we would like to further this discussion in this chapter on critical and analytical skills.

Who?

Let's start with *who*. So the question here is *who* has made the assertion that the above example is in fact accurate? Discussions of how a reality is created are contextualised in both individual and societal contexts.

> Black people have similar rates of common mental health problems as other ethnic groups and yet this census shows that they are 44 per cent more likely to be sectioned under the Mental Health Act ... and ... black men are 29 per cent more likely than average to be subjected to control and restraint. (MIND, 2005, cited in Quinney, 2006: 74)

This statement is based on information from the health census, so if you are thinking of exploring this particular topic, you will need to think about the academic quality of this initial source and who it has been compiled by and, importantly, who is using the information to support a specific position. MIND is a well-established and respected mental health charity that funds research into many areas of mental health, so the next question you may wish to think about is whether the statement from the health census is supported with independent research that has been commissioned from other sources. Looking at the potential racial understanding of the researchers may also have significance, along with the inclusion (or not) of the perspectives of people who use the services that are being examined. For instance, it may be useful to explore the views and experiences of black men who have been detained under the Mental Health Act and restrained following the detention.

Looking in more detail at the concepts expressed in the statement from MIND, it may also be relevant to start to explore the problems of over-simplifying the position of black men as if they are passive recipients of treatment. It may be useful to explore some theoretical frameworks that offer explanations of the value of looking at the experiences of individuals and how their understanding of the world is shaped by a wide range of factors. Social constructivism (Lee and Greene, 2009) is one such theoretical framework as it values the individual's reality and recognises that this is influenced by individual and societal influences.

As Teater (2010: 83) defines:

> Social constructivism is a theory that values each person's reality as being uniquely shaped by her or his environment, culture, society, history, developmental processes and cognitions.

Taking a social constructivist view of the over-representation of black men in restrictive mental health services offers some discussion on the impact of society on the individual and the negative stereotyping of men in this group.

In looking at more complex explanations of the topic, you will be starting on the path of discovering which other writers have published in your topic area.

When?

It is relevant to your understanding and analysis of the research to look at *when* it was carried out, as well as looking at who did the research. For instance, if the literature that you are considering has been written for a specific purpose (e.g. government guidance or a serious case review), then the timing of the published work will be relevant. You need to consider the age (date) of the literature too, in order to place the literature within the wider societal expectations and understandings at that given point in time. For example, our understanding of the impact of institutional racism has been highlighted over the last two decades in the UK following the murder of Stephen Lawrence.

In April 1993 a young black British man, Stephen Lawrence, was stabbed to death at a bus stop in an unprovoked, racist attack. The police at the time were seriously criticised for their conduct of the investigation. After a sustained campaign from Stephen's parents about the police response, a judicial inquiry was set up by the then UK Home Secretary, Jack Straw. The inquiry was chaired by Sir William Macpherson and it was his report, published in 1999, that first identified the levels of institutional racism in the Metropolitan Police Force.

As well as looking at when a piece of work is commissioned, it is also important to look at the professional background and experience of the author(s). Macpherson's report clearly evidenced the level of institutional racism in the Metropolitan Police and also provided a detailed examination of the value base of the police that led to a restructuring of the training and induction of newly appointed police officers. So the timing of the publication of the literature for your review will be worthy of exploration and explanation.

The political context may also be significant in relation to looking at the timings of both the initial report and the subsequent findings of the Home Affairs Committee (2009), which was appointed to review the original Macpherson report (1999). Ten years on from his first report, the update looked at the progress that had been made by the police in relation to his original recommendations. In the update there were some positive developments in relation to the implementation of recommendations, but also some concern about the remaining overly disproportionate representation of black people in the stop-and-search statistics and on the National DNA Database, and that the gap in racial terms had widened since the first Macpherson report ten years earlier.

We have looked here at the importance of when a publication was written to highlight how excluding either of the reports from Macpherson would present an inaccurate commentary on the progress and understanding of institutional racism. If we had only considered the first report in 1999 from Macpherson, then we would have missed some significant findings that were highlighted by the Home Affairs Committee ten years later. Any critical analysis of only the first report would have been limited without a consideration of the findings of the later publication. A key message here is not only *when* the publication was written, but also *how many* other related and relevant publications have followed the original one.

Where?

Looking at where the research that informs the literature has taken place will be informative to your review. For example, looking at the academic discipline in which the research was conducted will inform the context of the research and indeed may give you insight into the historical exploration of the topic and also some understanding of the academic credibility of the work.

The geographic context may also be relevant, and understanding the demographic profile of the subjects of the research can also inform your analysis of the literature on your chosen topic. The international credibility of published work will also be helpful in your discussion of the work as part of your literature review.

The location of research is important, as is where the work is published. We have already discussed that the importance of peer-reviewed academic work is undisputed, but it is also important to view all relevant sources. As McLaughlin (2012) suggests, there is a need for caution in disregarding work from less well known journals, although articles published in more prestigious ones do often contain work of a high academic quality.

Why?

Asking *why* a piece of work has been commissioned and undertaken by particular researchers at a particular point in time will be a searching question for you as you begin to digest the scope and detail of your topic area. If we refer back to Macpherson's work on institutional racism in relation to the death of Stephen Lawrence, then the question 'why?' is answered in the reason that the report was first commissioned. Concerns about the lack of a speedy police response to the investigation of the murder of this young man caused a public outcry, and his family raised the profile of his treatment through the media. The Macpherson Report (1999) was the result of the judicial inquiry commissioned in response to the failures that had been highlighted in respect of the attitude of the investigating officers. So the 'why?' of this particular publication was very transparent, but other publications may not be so obvious. It is in discussion with your literature review supervisor that you will be able to explore the historical context of your topic, which may inform the reason for the publication in the first instance.

Another 'why?' question may be to consider how far a government publication such as the Macpherson Report can be regarded as a credible piece of research. It may well be relevant to your literature review as a publication, but it is important to remember the remit of the judicial inquiry and the subsequent findings.

Your confidence in searching through the who, when, where and why can become the building blocks of your increased confidence in looking at bias and academic credibility.

Received Wisdom and Dissenting Voices

A significant part of your discussion of the literature that you have drawn upon will be looking at the received wisdom alongside any other work that challenges the findings and assertions of the literature that you have selected at the first stage of your review. If we continue to explore the statement from MIND, the mental health charity, in respect of black British men and the over-representation of this group in detention under the Mental Health Act, then we can look to more detailed explanations of inequality. These explanations of inequality will no doubt be a part of your qualifying and post-qualifying studies in social work. This understanding will also be informed by application in your practice of the value base that the social work profession is proud to showcase. But what of the dissenting voices? It is important to remember that dissenting voices do not necessarily mean opposite views, but can and do include views that take a different position but are not diametrically opposed. For example, an understanding of the experiences of black British men in the mental health system, with a specific emphasis on culture and race, has been discussed by Fernando (2010), who provides a key to the complexity of the subject.

Drawing together the connections between the publications that you have read, the comments from MIND (2005) on the health census, and the exploration into institutional racism in the police from the Macpherson reports (Macpherson, 1999; House of Commons Home Affairs Committee, 2009) will give you the opportunity to widen and deepen your appreciation of the complexity of the topic of race, mental health and institutional racisms.

An important part of the discussion of the literature will hinge on your ability to present any areas of bias and academic credibility. There are some key pitfalls to avoid in relation to bias and academic credibility. McGee (2010) comprehensively lists the common errors or fallacies to avoid. These include: over-generalisation, limited knowledge, reliance on tradition, and lack of evidence from peer-reviewed sources. This area of bias and academic credibility will be informed by the quality and depth of your reading and also by your willingness to look openly at the opposite positions to the arguments that you present.

Understanding the bias in a published piece of work is a challenge for the beginning critical thinker and you may find that a peer-reviewed piece of work does not ensure a lack of bias from the reviewer(s). As McLaughlin (2012) highlights, the process of peer review does not ensure that the quality of the work is assured:

> There are however limitations to the peer-review process as the peer reviewers may have established perspectives or paradigmatic views that may act as a barrier to publishing new or alternative perspectives. (McLaughlin, 2012: 116)

Skills for Critical Thinking and Analysis

GOOD NEWS – as a qualified social worker you will already have some of these skills, and if you are a student studying on a qualifying course you will be well on your way to acquiring them.

A one-sided view?

Select three publications from your chosen topic area and present a one-sided discussion of the arguments. Limit yourself to 250 words for each publication. Now quickly sketch out

(Continued)

ACTIVITY

(Continued)

your first thoughts regarding the counter-arguments to these one-sided views. Use spider diagrams to show how your thoughts connect.

Present the more detailed one-sided views (250 words) and then the quick thoughts in the spider diagram as a basis for a discussion of the complexities of the topic with your review supervisor.

A literature review demands a critical appraisal and logical analysis of the selected material in the same way as the information you process in your social work practice. Whether you are preparing a case record or report for a review, conference or court, you will have gathered the information, usually from a variety of sources, and will be required to order the facts logically. You will then play a part in the provision of an evidence-based professional opinion while paying careful attention to both the accuracy and relevance of the information that you have gathered. As the social worker, you will also be required to record any disagreements from the sources about the accuracy of the content. These tasks require a range of skills, from listening to critical analysis, and in between you will have used your ability to listen, to absorb, to record, to summarise and to evaluate. Professionally, you will also want to ensure that you process the information objectively and logically, and that the way you handle it meets the value requirements of social work practice.

Let us look in more detail at how the processing of information in practice will be relevant to the critical analysis that you will use in your literature review. The ability to think critically and objectively is a key skill that has been recognised in both social work education and practice. In social work education, the Quality Assurance Agency (QAA), which has benchmarked the standards for UK social work courses, clearly identify that:

> Social work is a moral activity that requires practitioners to recognise the dignity of the individual, but also to make and implement difficult decisions (including restriction of liberty) in human situations that involve the potential for benefit or harm.
>
> Honours degree programmes in social work therefore involve the study, application of, and critical reflection upon, ethical principles and dilemmas. (Quality Assurance Agency (QQA), 2008: 4.6, cited in McLaughlin, 2012: 53)

Reflection and Critical Thinking

In social work practice the skill of critical analysis is recognised in relation to reflecting and thinking critically. Reflection for a social worker is the ability to maintain a confident understanding of the self in relation to feelings, observations and knowledge that in turn informs our understanding of the service users who access services. The reflective practitioner has been defined by Schön (1991), who suggests that the reflective practitioner needs to look reflectively at theories and knowledge to develop ways of understanding emotions and behaviours in order to work creatively within human relationships. Reflection in action is defined as reflexivity, as Sheppard (1998) describes:

The notion of reflexivity emphasises the social worker (i) as an active thinker, able to assess, respond and initiate action and (ii) as a social actor who actually participates in the situation with which they are concerned in the conduct of their practice.

Thus the reflective practitioner, in practical terms, is one who is aware of the socially situated relationship with their client(s), i.e. with a clear understanding of their role and purpose; who understands themselves as a participant whose actions and interactions are part of the social work process; who is capable of analysing situations and evidence, with an awareness of the way their own participation affects this process; who is able to identify the intellectual and practice processes involved in assessment and intervention; who is aware of the assumptions underlying the ways they 'make sense' of practice situations; and who is able to do so in relation to the nature and purposes of their practice. (Sheppard, 1998: 767, cited in Trevithick, 2007: 46)

The way in which you will be given the opportunity to develop this reflexivity is initially through supervision with your practice supervisor and, in the context of your literature review, with your academic supervisor. Please see below for some guidance on how to achieve the most in supervision sessions, which will focus on the development of your critical thinking in your literature review. The conscious reworking and deconstructing of academic positions and discussions will enable you to really review the literature that you have chosen to consider in the context of your chosen topic.

The discussion of the material that you select is the starting point of your critical analysis. It may be that, through seminar groups or tutorials, you are given the opportunity to debate the concepts within the literature that you have selected.

Think about... Recording your discussion with your literature review supervisor

The sessions you have with your review supervisor will need to be written up to enable you to refer back to them and to use the discussions as a learning tool. The discussions on both your content and progress can form a helpful building block to inform the analysis in your literature review. Brief notes may suffice, but it will be a wasted opportunity if you let the words of wisdom (both yours and those of your supervisor) disappear into the ether.

You will certainly have the opportunity to discuss the concepts with your review supervisor and it is in these discussions that you will have the benefit of testing out your interpretations of the literature. Although these discussions will not be formal debates in the traditional sense, they will give you the opportunity to see the different arguments presented in the literature and also to gain a view of how diverse the interpretation of academic literature can be from different individual perspectives.

Critical analysis comes from the ability to question and look logically at the information that you are reviewing so attention to detail and accuracy are both important aspects of your approach and will have a particular relevance. Again, these are social work skills and are often used in direct work with service users when working towards empowerment. The deconstruction of perceptions can be particularly positive in work with service users who have been disempowered, and the deconstruction of perceptions in social work practice is used in enabling a service user to reframe overly negative self-assumptions. Teater (2010: 62) explores this in relation to the use of language:

> *Language of elaboration and clarification.* Encouraging clients to elaborate and clarify situations allows for social workers and clients to fully explore the clients' stories and the evidence for and against their current belief systems.

Elder (2009) presents a number of helpful questions to consider in looking analytically at specific literature:

- What is the author's fundamental purpose?
- What is the author's point of view?
- What assumptions is the author making in his or her reasoning?
- What are the implications of these assumptions?
- What information does the author use in reasoning throughout the text?
- What are the most fundamental inferences or conclusions used in the text?
- What are the basic concepts used?
- What is the key question the author is trying to answer? (cited in Cocker and Allain, 2011: 20–21)

The above questions provide a framework to structure your reading of a piece of literature, and looking at the purpose of the writing may well include consideration of how the piece has been commissioned. If it is based on specific research, asking who has undertaken and funded the research may well be relevant. Looking at the assumptions of the writer will also inform your critical analysis and enable you to consider again the question of bias that we discussed earlier in this chapter. A consideration of the information and sources used to support the written piece will also guide you in how the writer has reasoned the discussion and formulated the arguments.

Chapter Summary

- In this chapter we have asked you to consider the context of the literature that you have selected to review.
- We have encouraged you to consider the key factors of who has written the work and the timing of the writing.
- We have asked you to look at where and why the work was written.
- We have given an example of the relevance of looking in a detailed way at publications and to view them as part of a wider context, with special consideration of any follow-up work that may impact on your review.
- We have identified how your existing practice skills of reflection relate to your critical analysis skills.
- We have examined the importance of looking at the range of arguments that surround your chosen topic, especially in relation to the inclusion of dissenting voices.

- We have encouraged you to consider the significance of the author(s) and to look critically at the range of publications and the quality of the academic work within them.

Further Reading and Useful Resources

Elder, L. (2009) 'I think critically, therefore I am', *Times Higher Education*, 6 August. Available at: www.timeshighereducation.co.uk/features/i-think-critically-therefore-i-am/407700.article (This article describes a lecturer's epiphany in relation to critical thinking, and how it altered the way she nurtured this skill within her students.)

McLaughlin, H. (2012) *Understanding Social Work Research*. London: Sage. (This book gives a comprehensive guide to critical thinking in the context of social work research, along with some very helpful practice examples.)

Oko, J. (2008) *Understanding and Using Social Work Theory*. Exeter: Learning Matters. (In this book the author links the skills of critical thinking and reflection to social work practice, highlighting the importance of them in the decision-making processes that social workers undertake in practice.)

References

Elder, L. (2009) 'I think critically, therefore I am', *Times Higher Education*, 6 August. Available at: www.timeshighereducation.co.uk/features/i-think-critically-therefore-i-am/407700.article. Also cited in Cocker, C. and Allain, L. (2011) *Advanced Social Work with Children and Families*. Exeter: Learning Matters, pp. 20–21.

Fernando, S. (2010) *Mental Health, Race and Culture*. Basingstoke: Palgrave Macmillan.

House of Commons Home Affairs Committee (2009) *The Macpherson Report – Ten Years On*. London: The Stationery Office. Available at: www.publications.parliament.uk/pa/cm200809/cmselect/cmhaff/427/42703.htm (accessed 15 November 2012).

Jesson, J., with Matheson, L. and Lacey, F.M. (2011) *Doing Your Literature Review: Traditional and Systematic Techniques*. London: Sage.

Lee, M.Y. and Greene, G.J. (2009) 'Using social constructivism in social work practice', in A.R. Roberts (ed.), *The Social Workers' Desk Reference* (2nd edition). New York: Oxford University Press.

Macpherson, Sir W. (1999) The Stephen Lawrence Enquiry (The Macpherson Report). London: Home Office. Available at: www.archive.official-documents.co.uk/document/cm42/4262/4262.htm (accessed 12 December 2012).

McGee, S. (2010) *Key Research Skills in Psychology*. London: Sage.

McLaughlin, H. (2012) *Understanding Social Work Research*. London: Sage.

MIND (2005) 'Census supports *Mind* concerns over racism in NHS'. Available at: www.mind.org.uk (accessed 15 November 2012).

Quinney, A. (2006) *Collaborative Social Work Practice*. Exeter: Learning Matters.

Schön, D. (1991) *The Reflective Practitioner: How Professionals Think in Action*. Aldershot: Arena.

Teater, B. (2010) *An Introduction to Applying Social Work Theories and Methods*. New York: Oxford University Press.

Trevithick, P. (2007) *Social Work Skills: A Practice Handbook* (2nd edition). Maidenhead: Open University Press.

7

Strategies for Effective Note-taking

☑ **Learning Outcomes** ☑

- To clarify the professional skills in note-taking
- To look at how you will summarise complex information
- To recognise the importance of using your own words in note-taking
- To clarify the relevant information to include in your notes
- To prioritise the recording of your sources

Some Key Questions to Think about

- Why take notes?
- What skills are involved in note-taking?
- What knowledge is required?
- What do you already know about note-taking?
- What skills do you already have/use in note-taking?
- What types of notes are needed for your literature review?

Why Take Notes?

The main reason for taking notes is so that they can assist you to produce your own individual piece of work that is accurately based on the theoretical knowledge and critical analysis of writers who have published in your chosen subject area. The notes will form the evidence base for your discussion and will demonstrate that your work has been produced in a thoroughly considered and academically credible way. Although you may have some lively ideas about the subject you have chosen, you will need to demonstrate that your ideas have been supported and/or challenged by the academic writers who have written and published in this subject area. Drawing on the established and peer-reviewed knowledge base will provide you with the building blocks for your own final literature review.

Theoretical knowledge in social work has become recognised as an important part of social work practice, which is informed by evidence. The academic work that you do for your literature review will help to inform your own evidence-based practice. The importance of demonstrating the knowledge base of evidence to support professional understanding has been showcased in the Munro Review (Munro, 2011). Your literature review is not only the academic starting point for the extension of your understanding, but also a base on which to anchor your developing repertoire of social work theory.

In order to meet the requirements of your literature review you will need to read extensively – much more than your word allowance will permit you to write. The range of your reading will demonstrate your wider understanding and, as such, will contribute to the academic credibility of your work. Summarising the material will be an important part of making useful and accurate notes. Looking at key concepts and keywords will assist in note-taking, but a core requirement is that you have fully understood what you are reading. If there are areas that puzzle you, then make a note of them and look to further research and/or discuss them with your academic supervisor.

The evidence base for your work from other academic sources will also provide you with the platform to examine them critically and analytically. In this respect, it is important to establish from the start a critical approach to your note-taking. With regards to the age of the work, for example, if you are looking at a social work text that has been written before concepts of multiple attachments in children were developed, then you will, by nature of the date of the text, be reading works that present you with a partial and dated picture. In his early work, Bowlby (1958) focused on the significance of the *mother* as the key attachment figure, but in later work he recognised the importance of the *significant caregiver* as an important attachment figure who could play an equally important part in the child's emotional health as any other carer. The later work on attachment was developed further by Bowlby (1998) and later by Rutter (cited in McLeod, 2007), who reviewed the progression of the studies on attachment from the initial findings by Bowlby. Thus, in this example, we see a topic that has been developed and discussed over a period of more than 50 years. This will give you an indication of the time span that your note-taking will need to consider. Recognising at the outset that a subject has been developed over time will be the start of your critical approach to note-taking, which will be enhanced by your acknowledgement of the significance of the date of the publications that you have chosen to review.

Another reason to take notes is a very practical one, as you will be researching material that will, as we have established, far exceed the word limit of your finished piece of work. So, in order to ensure that you have considered the total depth and breadth of the subject, you will be looking at significant amounts of written material. This will involve a skilled sifting process of condensing the amount of material that you have looked at in order to meet the required word limit of your individual piece of work. As a social worker or social work student, you will be developing your skills of processing information in both written and verbal contexts, so this sifting process is one that will closely connect to your professional practice base. The discipline of keeping to the prescribed word limit is relevant because you will be required to write in this way as a social worker/student, for example in initial referrals, court reports, review reports, assessments, and in many more cases.

The last but probably the most important reason for taking notes is to assist you in developing your understanding of the literature that you are reviewing. This will be facilitated through the development of your summarising and reframing skills in order to present your own understanding of the material that you are using. A part of this sifting will include a very open approach to recording the information that you are struggling to understand. Obviously you will be accessing new areas of knowledge as part of your review, and it is important that you have a system of taking notes that clearly highlights any areas that you will need to study further and in greater depth so that you fully understand the content.

It is only when you have read widely that you will be able to contemplate the breadth and depth of your subject area. Then you will be in an informed position to determine the most relevant and interesting works that you want to review.

What Skills are Involved in Note-taking?

You may already have experience of taking notes in a professional setting and this may be as a student or qualified social worker – perhaps where you have been interviewing a service user or carer and needed to record the content of your discussion. If this is true in your case, you will no doubt have identified the practical skills involved in note-taking. In some ways the social work interview can be easier to define and record than the academic note-taking that you will be asked to do as part of your literature review. This is because usually in a social work interview you will have been asked to undertake a specific task or gather information in order to collate the views of the person/people that you are interviewing. (We know that you will be very familiar with situations where a referral has given you one piece of information and you quickly find out that the situation you are presented with bears little or no resemblance to that initial request.)

The starting point for your literature review may not be clear and you may be faced with information that you need to understand and digest into notes that will ultimately help you to understand your chosen subject area, and then to produce a relevant and critical review of the literature that you have examined.

It is important that you construct your notes in your own personal style that is totally understandable to you so that you can use them when you start to formally write up your literature review. You may, for example, have been in lectures where you found the speaker really interesting, only to discover that you have been too interested in listening and have not written enough notes to help you recall the content at a later point.

The 'light-bulb moment' could be that through your own self-awareness (or from absolute frustration about having inaccurate notes!) you have identified a skill that you need to work on. Perhaps the following questions may be useful:

1. Were you too interested in listening and weighing up the information to think about taking notes?
2. Did you feel distracted from listening by having to work out what to note down so the end result was totally different from the content?
3. Did you understand the content enough to write notes that would assist you when the lecture had finished?

If any of the above sounds familiar to you, this may be the perfect starting point for that initial appointment with your tutor before you pick up your note-taking pen or keyboard!

We would like to offer some suggestions to encourage you in the note-taking that you are about to undertake. Recognising the importance of being prepared in practical terms with writing materials and ideally some head-space to concentrate are good starting points. Thinking about how you will listen to the lecture or tune in to the written material will also help you to make the most of the information. The skill of selecting the most relevant material will be enhanced by your existing knowledge and previous reading in the chosen subject area.

Skills in Note-taking – Some Suggestions

- Preparation
- Listening or tuning in
- Sifting and analysing information
- Writing clearly

Mind maps

Mind maps can be helpful in organising your note-taking and the starting point is to map out the subject area that you want to review. For example, if the subject for review is to look at a specific area of Child Protection then you will need to draw this in the centre of your map. The branches that come from the centre will represent the keywords that you have identified as the starting point for your review, such as knowledge, practice, risk and legal aspects. Along with the keywords, add an approximate number of the words to be recorded in note form. The keywords with the approximate numbers will guide you in the areas that you need to explore and make clear how much note-taking you need to complete to record your reading. Mind maps can help you to look in detail at the breakdown of the word limit for your work – for example, 1000 words of notes may represent 1500–2000 of finished writing.

As part of your task in preparing the ground for your literature review, you will be involved in the process of sifting through large amounts of written material that you have identified as relevant to your chosen topic. The recognition of relevant materials is neither easy nor straightforward, and it is likely that you will have some angst around the final choice of the works you want to consider. One useful way of checking that you have identified the most relevant areas that are pertinent to your topic is the use of mind maps. This is a technique that you may have used in previous study settings. It can be a useful tool to establish both the content and the context of your chosen area.

Buzan (2009) saw the mind map as a two-dimensional tool that allows you to consider a subject in its broadest and most specific context. The idea is that you would use a diagram to map out the key areas of your subject, such as if you were looking at the subject of attachment in the case study of Nina which follows.

Nina

You have been given the following case scenario and have been asked to look at published research and knowledge on the concept of attachment with a plan to complete a literature review.

Nina is 8 years old and has been a 'looked-after child' since the age of 2 when she was made subject of a Care Order. Nina has had three different foster placements but has been unable to settle in any of them. Her present carers, Lena and Fred, have asked for support from social services because they are trying to support Nina to make sense of the numerous moves that she has experienced.

You are a first-year undergraduate student who has just started studying on the 'Preparation for practice' module, which includes a particular emphasis on developing your knowledge and understanding on the concept of attachment. Lena and Fred are worried about Nina, who seems to be very unhappy. Nina has suddenly started to run away from school but has not been able to talk about why she is unhappy.

How do you think an understanding of attachment would help you to understand Nina and her situation?

You have very little experience of looking at the knowledge base on attachment and, because of this, think that you need to start from scratch. Some of your first thoughts about Nina could be:

- Where do I start?
- What exactly is attachment?
- Why do social workers need to know about attachment?
- How does it connect to day-to-day practice?
- Is attachment only relevant if working with children and families?
- Does attachment connect to the legal requirements in social work?
- Does age, race, culture and class impact on attachment?
- Where do I find the information I need to answer the above questions?

The main subject may be ATTACHMENT but the subdivisions would include the IMPACT on a child of Nina's age and a consideration of SIGNIFICANT CAREGIVERS and issues of IDENTITY. Another main subject area in understanding Nina's world may be in relation to CHILD DEVELOPMENT and the age-appropriate milestones that could be expected of a child of her age, along with some of the significant EMOTIONAL and PRACTICAL considerations of the many moves that she experienced as a 'looked-after child'. Using a mind map as part of the preparation for the note-taking could offer the opportunity to understand the context and breadth of the subject and help to guide you to the areas you need to research. Your initial note-taking could be focused on the subject areas that you identify in your mind map.

Mind maps are sometimes known as spray diagrams or concept maps, but the ideas are very similar and aim to provide a starting point to help you to locate the key areas of the subject that you have chosen to review. Mind maps will highlight the gaps in your knowledge, but they will also give you the opportunity to identify your existing understanding and knowledge base in the chosen subject area.

Listening and tuning in

You may think that the skills of listening and note-taking seem a bit disconnected but let's go back to the 'light-bulb moment'. As a social worker or student social worker, you will be very familiar with the importance of the communication skills of listening, both in the context of professional social work requirements and from well established evidence-based knowledge in social work. One significant source that may be especially relevant, as it concentrates on improving practice, is the Munro Review of Child Protection, which highlighted gaps in relation to effective communication in practice (Munro, 2011).

Identifying the day-to-day listening skills that you use as a social worker will help you switch on to them when note-taking. Realising that you have the necessary listening skill may be the light bulb moment for you!

Now, how do you transfer your ability to listen and tune in in your professional practice with service users, carers and colleagues to the task of note-taking for your literature review? The first step is to consider the skill of listening that you use in practice, and this may well be one of 'active listening' (Hoppe, 2011).

For the purposes of the literature review, we need to consider listening in relation to both your experience in lectures and, most importantly, as to how you listen and tune in to yourself when you are reading a chosen text in your subject area. When you are actively listening to a person in a conversation you may have a clear discipline which focuses your attention. This focus ensures that the information that you are hearing is received and recorded accurately. Think about how, when you listen to a conversation, you are also tuning in to the context and the content of the information that you are hearing. However, this discipline may not be there when you are reading and the temptation to read but not record may be one of the areas you need to address. It is fair to say that if you are reading an academic text as part of your work on your literature review but not making notes, then you are probably wasting your time. Harsh words, I know, but the ability to retain pertinent parts of academic theory without the aid of notes has to be questionable. Applying your knowledge of listening and tuning in to your own reading will enhance the retention of the information, but if you are also making notes of the content at the same time, you will be developing a coherent approach to the work required to build your literature review.

Historically reading has been done both out loud to others or privately in the way that you will be very familiar with in relation to your work on your literature review. The way that you are able to 'listen' to the information when reading privately will play a significant part in the quality of your written notes.

The actual content of many social work texts can be both disturbing and challenging to read, and this is evident in any work on Serious Case Reviews that you may want to examine in relation to a specific literature review. The difficult content can impact upon our ability 'to listen to' or 'tune in to' the information we are reading, and as such may impact on our openness to record the content in the notes we need to take. The following case study considers a subject area that we may find challenging to 'listen to' and 'tune in to' in our note-taking.

You have just started on a Master's degree in Social Work, following your first undergraduate degree in Psychology. You are really keen to become a qualified social worker and eventually want to work in a children and family setting. You have identified a project with your tutor as part of the 'Safeguarding' module that is studied as part of placement preparation before you go out on your first period of assessed practice.

The module has a specific learning outcome of enabling you to look critically at research findings that will inform your social work practice. A real emphasis is on developing your critical awareness and knowledge about research informed by evidence-based practice. Your particular project will focus on the findings and lessons learned from the Serious Case Reviews into child deaths.

Some first thoughts on this problem may be:

- What is the history of Serious Case Reviews?
- What is evidence-based practice?
- Why do social workers need to provide evidence to support their practice?
- How do I develop my critical skills when I read about new knowledge and understandings in this area?
- What is the social work role in safeguarding children?
- How does this role fit with the other professionals involved in safeguarding?
- How much are children and parents included in the evidence on which practice is based for social work?
- How can I use my note-taking skills of listening and tuning in to help me to make sense of this subject area?

The questions we have posed encourage you to look at the wide range of considerations in relation to Serious Case Reviews. You will need to be faced with a large amount of information and it may be useful for you to look at how you can sift through it in order to understand both the content and the relevance. We discuss some aspects of sifting information in the next section.

Sifting and analysing information

When you are reading a work and taking notes it can be helpful to consider the importance of making sure that you understand the content. If the information seems inaccessible to you, think about how you will record what you have not fully understood. You may need to decide exactly how you will record the need for further explanation in the specific area that you may be unsure about. Below are some ideas on how to approach this task:

- You may choose to use abbreviations or keywords and phrases, such as SCRs (Serious Case Reviews), CP (child protection), CYP (children & young people), FS (family services, 89Act (1989 Children Act)) and CPC (Child Protection Case Conference) as marginal reminders to yourself to investigate further.
- You may choose to ask yourself questions, such as: Why, how and when was this written? Has anyone else developed this more recently?
- Much more simply, you may record the keywords that you do not understand. One very simple tip to identify the troublesome words may be to have a margin

on each page that is especially reserved for words or concepts that you know you will need to explore in more detail.

- Another consideration is to look at the amount of information that you are reading and try to determine if the format or content is difficult for you to comprehend and to adopt the 'chunking' technique (Miller et al., 1960) described next.

Miller et al. (1960) first defined the concept of 'chunking' in relation to written communication between human beings, focusing on the formula 'The magical number seven, plus or minus two'. They suggested that most people can remember about seven recently learnt chunks of similarly classified data, plus or minus two. They concluded that this number was the 'chunking limit' for understanding, but that this number significantly reduced when the information increased in complexity. When reading and note-taking information for your literature review, it may be interesting to test yourself against the 'seven plus or minus two' formula that Miller et al. devised and apply it to your work.

Processing your information

A significant part of the note-taking will be the processing of the information that you are reading for your review. The processing will include reading the material in a critical way and asking some relevant questions of the text (which refers back to Chapter 6 where we looked at who, what when and where?) These questions will help you to look critically at the content of the material that you are taking notes on as part of gathering the relevant information for your literature review:

- Who is the author and when was it written?
- What are the keywords you have identified in the mind map?
- How many words in the main body of your review will the notes inform?
- Have you identified a system of abbreviations that assists you when taking notes and, more importantly, that makes sense to you when you look back at them?

If your note-taking starts in a broad sweep of the subject and hones down to more specific topics, you will have both a context and overview of the chosen subject area. If you have experienced problems in making sense of your notes in the past, it may be that you have been too general in the recording and have not concentrated on enough specific detail.

Chapter Summary

- In this chapter we have explored why we take notes.
- We have looked at the skills involved in accurate note-taking.
- We have emphasised the relevance of looking at the timescale of publications on your topic.
- We have considered case studies to guide keywords and concepts.

Further Reading and Useful Resources

The following resources will provide some interesting ideas on the theories that look to explain how information is processed and they may also help you to identify how you process the information that you access as part of your literature review.

George A. Miller, Information Processing – www.lifecircles-inc.com/Learningtheories/IP/GAMiller.html

McLeod, S.A. (2007) *Simply Psychology: Articles for Students*. Available at: www.simply psychology.org/ (accessed 12 December 2012).

www.simplypsychology.org/bowlby.html (Web page explaining Bowlby's theory of attachment which relates to the examples used in this chapter.)

References

Bowlby, J. (1958) 'The nature of a child's tie to his mother', *International Journal of Psychoanalysis*, 39: 350–71.

Bowlby, J. (1998) *Attachment and Loss, Sadness and Depression*. London: Pimlico.

Buzan, T. (2009) *The Mind Map Book: Unlock Your Creativity, Boost Your Memory*. Change Life. BBC Archive.

Hoppe, M.A. (2011) *Active Listening: Improve Your Ability to Listen and Lead*. Oxford: Wiley.

McLeod, S.A. (2007) *Simply Psychology: Articles for Students*. Available at: www.simply psychology.org/ (accessed 12 December 2012).

Miller, G., Pribran, K. and Galanter, E. (1960) *Plans and the Structure of Behavior*. New York: Holt, Reinhart & Winston.

Munro, E. (2011) *The Munro Review of Child Protection: Final Report, a Child-centred System*. London: The Stationery Office (TSO).

8

Writing Your Literature Review

☑ Learning Outcomes ☑

- To consider the planning issues that you should consider before beginning to write
- To develop an understanding about the different sections of the literature review and the kinds of things you need to write about in them
- To identify some practical tools that may help you to overcome difficulties encountered when writing your literature review
- To reflect on the value and importance of editing, redrafting and proofreading as key parts of the writing process

Planning to Write

Before you even begin the writing process, take a little time to think about the following issues:

- Word counts/limits (how much do you need to write?)

  o Help you plan roughly how much you should aim to write in each section of your review.
  o Give you a sense of how much detail you will be able to include.

- Submission dates (how much time do you have?)

  o Help you plan the best use of your writing time.

QUICK TIP: Set your own buffer deadline!
  Set your own deadlines for at least a few days in advance of the REAL deadline. This 'buffer time' will give you a bit of breathing space if anything unexpected happens (for instance, computer or printer problems, family or work crises).

Scheduling (best times to write?)

Writing can be slow and time-consuming so it's helpful to think realistically and creatively about when you can schedule writing times.

QUICK TIP: Short bursts!

Don't always put off writing until you think you have a decent chunk of time to use. Think about how you could break your writing time up into short sections. It's amazing how much can be written in even just a 15-minute chunk of time, and it can free you up and stop you from becoming nervous or perfectionist about your work.

Location (best place for you to write?)

For instance:

- Will the place allow me to work without distraction or disturbance?
- Do I have access to the resources I need?
- Is the environment comfortable for me to work in?
- **How will I stay motivated and deal with boredom and frustration?** Consider some of the strategies below or, even better, identify some that you know have worked for you in the past.

QUICK TIP: Boredom busters!

Plan and take regular breaks

- Try to keep a clear division between work and leisure time.
- Make time for physical activity and/or exercise – it can do wonders for your motivation and sense of well-being.
- Refuse to allow yourself to be constantly distracted by social media.
- Give yourself small rewards for tasks that you complete.

Planning your Literature Review

As with any piece of written work that you are producing, it's essential to begin with a clear plan of what you are intending to write. In the case of literature reviews, you will normally find that you are obliged to work with a pre-given review structure, whether that is provided by your academic department (if applicable) or, perhaps, the requirements of a body such as the Social Care Institute for Excellence or the Campbell Collaboration if you are writing a systematic review. It is therefore vital that you read the appropriate guidance about how the literature review should be structured in order to ensure that the completed piece of work is fit for purpose. We will discuss what is written in some of the key parts of literature reviews later in this chapter.

Irrespective of how the literature review needs to be structured, you will still face the task of how to organise your thoughts, ideas and arguments in a manner that has a logical flow. There are different techniques that you can use to help you structure your material, including the simple but effective 'ideas cluster' approach described below.

Create 'ideas clusters'

Ideas clusters are simply groupings of related ideas or concepts. They are useful because they can suggest sub-topics which may then become the focus of a paragraph or section of your literature review. To create ideas clusters:

- Briefly list all of the key points, topics, arguments and perspectives that relate to your literature review topic.
- Use a second document or sheet of paper to group together points which are related (i.e. create clusters).
- Rank these clusters in terms of the order in which they should be dealt with (for instance, it may be more logical to deal with one sub-topic before another).
- Use your ranked ideas clusters to help you put together an outline structure for your literature review.

Other ways of organising your material are outlined in the section below on 'the main body' of the literature review.

What Do You Write about in a Literature Review?

Think about... The writing up process

When you are ready to write up your work, you have one major task: how do you adequately, appropriately and interestingly describe, explain and justify what you have done and found out? (Hart, 1998: 172)

So, how do you actually go about doing this describing, explaining and justifying? Table 8.1 provides some of our prompts and ideas about what these processes involve.

Table 8.1   Some prompts and ideas about describing, explaining and justifying

	Could be addressed by:
Describe (Give an account of something)	Describing the range of coverage the topic has in the literature Describing the approach that has been taken to researching the topic in terms of approach (methodology) and tools (methods) Describing the key issues that crop up Describing what the main findings are Describing areas of agreement and disagreement Describing what you think has been omitted (i.e. the gaps in knowledge)

(Continued)

	Could be addressed by:
Explain (Make something clear or 'shed light' on it)	Explaining why the topic is important and relevant to contemporary social work practice Explaining where you think the strengths and weaknesses of the literature lie Explaining how findings from different studies can be synthesised Explaining what the strengths and limitations are of your literature review methodology (e.g. searching, data extraction, synthesis and reporting) Explaining the capacity of the literature to make any claims about the effectiveness of social work practice/interventions Explaining the boundaries and limitations to any claims that could be made
Justify (Provide evidence and reasoning)	Justifying an informed opinion based on the available evidence, statistical information, case studies, examples and the informed opinions of others Justifying your choice of literature review methodology, in light of the strengths and weaknesses you explained in connection with them Justifying your choice of literature review topic. What were your reasons for choosing this? Justifying leaving out certain aspects of the topic Justifying any claims you might make about how research in your topic area is most effectively carried out Justifying any claims that could be made in connection with improvements to social work practice and associated interventions

Table 8.1 (Continued)

Hart states that you should do this describing, explaining and justifying in a way that is *adequate* (i.e. meets a basic set of requirements), *appropriate* (i.e. follows academic writing conventions) and *interesting* (e.g. novel, innovative or creative).

Writing the Review – A Section-by-section Overview

Acknowledgements

It is common for literature reviews to have a brief acknowledgements section at the beginning. This is where you would provide thanks to those who have provided help, support, guidance, feedback and perhaps personal support during the process.

Abstract (or summary, or executive summary)

In academic work the abstract refers to a very brief summary (usually somewhere between 250 and 300 words) of the literature review or research paper. Executive summaries fulfil the same role in relation to reports and may be up to 1,000 words depending on the length of the report. Normally they briefly outline the:

- topic under investigation
- method(s) of investigation
- theoretical and critical frameworks applied to the investigation
- results or findings
- key conclusion(s)

Although the abstract comes at the very beginning of your literature review, it is not unusual for authors to write the abstract when they have finished writing all other parts of their literature review. This makes it easier to write a clear, concise and accurate summary of what the literature review actually contains.

Tips for writing the abstract

Table 8.2 provides some tips for writing the abstract.

Table 8.2   Some tips for writing the abstract

	Tips include:
Selection What needs to be included?	Print out a spare copy of your literature review and go through with a highlighter pen, emphasising what you think are the key points. (You could do this electronically instead by using the highlighter tool in your word-processing software.) Summarise these key points as briefly as possible.
Concision How to capture the main points without going into fine detail?	Read your draft abstract and delete anything which is repeated or contains a depth of detail which is not strictly necessary for a good understanding of your review. Try verbally explaining the main aspects of your literature review to a friend who does not have a specialist understanding of social work. What are the key points that you notice yourself picking out?
Coherence Have you provided the reader with the basic 'story' of what you found through your literature review?	Think about the abstract as an ultra-short story about your literature review! Stories need a basic structure – your literature review 'story' will already have this, based on the logical order in which you carried out the different stages of the review. Ask someone who doesn't know much about your literature review to read your abstract. Did it make sense to them (even if they are not necessarily familiar with every word/concept)?
Relevance There should be nothing appearing in the abstract which is not later discussed in the literature review.	This is simply a case of compare and contrast. First, read your abstract and then, to make sure nothing 'extra', 'additional' or just 'waffly' and irrelevant crept in, check back through your literature review.

The art of abstraction

Test your own ability to compose a clear and concise abstract.

- Search for an academic article which contains an abstract (preferably an article which is not too long).
- Remove the abstract section *without* reading it.
- Read the article in its entirety (minus the abstract).
- Have a go at writing your own version of the abstract for the article you've just read. Restrict yourself to using no more than 300 words.
- Finally, compare your version of the abstract with the original abstract that appeared with the article. Were there any major differences?
- What personal learning points can you take away from this activity?

Introduction (aims and objectives)

The introduction for your literature review should aim to serve the same role as an introduction for any other essay or assignment. It should introduce the topic to the reader and provide an outline of the following:

- the nature, purpose and scope of the review
- the aims and objectives of the review
- a brief introduction to your topic area and its significance or relevance
- a note making it clear to the reader why the topic you have chosen is important (perhaps you are looking at an issue which is high on the political agenda or has been hotly debated in the media; maybe there has been a recent change in legislation, policy and/or practice, etc.). How did you come to choose or focus in on this particular topic?
- a flavour of what's to come later in the literature review but without getting bogged down in the fine details at this stage.

Methodology

This section is where you provide a detailed account of the review methodology that you've used within your literature review. Some students struggle with this section because in response to the question, 'How did you go about doing your literature

Table 8.3   Examples of some of the choices you make in undertaking literature reviews

Search method(s):	What kind of approach did you use to literature searching? What were your reasons for taking this approach? Did you use any specialist techniques (e.g. Boolean searching) and data sources (e.g. ASSIA, Cochrane)? What worked well and what was less effective? Was there any user/stakeholder involvement in planning and development?

Inclusion/exclusion criteria	What were the criteria that you used to decide whether something needed to be included or not? Where did your criteria come from? Did a specific piece of work, idea or theory help you to develop your criteria?
Theoretical tools or critical perspectives used	Did you find that a particular theoretical view or model was useful in helping you make evaluations or judgements about other work? Did your critical perspective change over time and, if so, why?
Limitations	What were the limitations of your methodological approach to the literature review? How might these have impacted on the nature and quality of your final review?

review?' they think 'well, I just got some books and journal articles from the library, did some web searching ... and just ... did it!' But you will have made lots of choices and decisions about how you carried out the review. Ask yourself some of the questions listed in Table 8.3.

Musing on methods

Time suggested: 20–30 minutes

Take a look at the following methodology section that has been taken from the publication *Informed Consent in Social Research: A Literature Review* by Wiles et al. (2005). Don't worry if you don't understand everything that the extract is talking about in terms of subject matter.

As you read the extract, answer the following questions:

- Which search methodologies have the reviewers used?
- Which search terms were used? Was this modified at all and, if so, for what reasons?
- What kinds of limits (if any) were placed on the search?
- Which criteria guided the review team in deciding what literature was relevant to their review?

Method

The literature review was conducted through searches of bibliographic databases as well as hand searching of journals and library searches of books. The following databases were searched: BIDS; Ingenta Select; Web of Science; ASSIA; EBSCO; Sociological Abstracts; and Social Services Abstracts. The initial terms used for the search were: 'informed consent', 'ethics', 'participation rates' and 'confidentiality'. The search was limited to the years 1998–2004. Many of the papers identified using these search terms related to medical studies and these were mostly discarded unless they were felt to have particular relevance to debates in social research. The search strategy was refined by including the term 'social research' to the search categories. The papers identified were checked for relevance. Those included were papers which addressed:

(Continued)

ACTIVITY

(Continued)

a) general literature relating to research ethics which have relevance to the principles surrounding consent;
b) general literature on informed consent in social research;
c) papers relating to the six specific areas focused on in the study in relation to informed consent – these included both consent in relation to substantive projects as well as discussions of consent more generally;
d) papers relating to consent to medical research or treatment which have relevance for consent in social research.

The reference lists of key papers identified through this process were also checked for relevant references. Hand searching of key journals in health (*Sociology of Health and Illness*), youth (*Journal of Youth Studies*) and social research methods (*International Journal of Social Research Methodology*) was also conducted. Papers or books referred to by researcher-participants in the ESRC project on informed consent were also included in the review. Books on research ethics were identified through library searches and cross-referencing papers. These included some of the key texts on this topic published prior to 1998. Research methods text-books published from 1995 were also checked. We identified 107 references from this search strategy. An annotated bibliography of these references can be found at:

www.sociologyandsocialpolicy.soton.ac.uk/Proj/Informed_Consent/index.htm

The main body (may incorporate results/findings and discussion)

This is the part of your literature review where you really begin to focus on providing an organised, balanced and critical overview of the published work relevant to the topic that you're discussing. The main body will sometimes also report on the results or findings from the review process, and the discussion of these results. In other contexts these may be separated out into discrete sections of the literature review.

Cronin et al. (2008) have adapted Carnwell and Daly's (2001) four approaches to framing the material in the literature review, in the form of a helpful table (Table 8.4).

Table 8.4   Four approaches to framing your literature review (Cronin et al., 2008, adapted from Carnwell and Daly, 2001)

Approach	Definition	Advantages/disadvantages
Dividing the literature into themes or categories	Distinct themes from the literature are discussed	Most popular approach Allows integration of theoretical and empirical (research) literature Care must be taken in ensuring that the themes are clearly related to the literature
Presenting the literature chronologically	Literature divided into time periods	Useful when examining the emergence of a topic over a period of time

Approach	Definition	Advantages/disadvantages
Exploring the theoretical and methodological literature	Discussion of theoretical literature followed by exploration of methodological literature that would give some indication of why a particular research design might be appropriate for investigating the topic	Useful when the body of literature is largely theoretical with little or no empirical (research) literature. Can be used to identify the need for qualitative studies
Examining theoretical literature and empirical literature in two sections	Where the topic has both theoretical and empirical literature and each is discussed separately	May tend to be a description rather than a critical review

Part of the skill involved in writing this section is to be able to select an appropriate 'frame' in order to discuss your particular topic.

Findings/results

This is the section of the review which draws together findings, results and/or thematic issues from the individual pieces of literature considered in the review process. In order to do this you will need to explain how data has been extracted and synthesised. We discussed some general points and approaches to these issues in Chapter 1. The findings/results section will vary with different types of literature review, with some featuring meta-analyses of quantitative data, others using a thematic approach to the analysis of qualitative data, and some using a mixture of approaches. The aim is to be as transparent as possible about how any data analysis and synthesis has been carried out.

Highlighting the limitations of the methods of data extraction and synthesis can be left until the 'discussion' section, and the implications of the findings/results should come in the 'conclusion' section.

Discussion

The discussion is where you 'discuss' the issues, complexities, anomalies, opportunities and problems that arose during the literature review process. It is a useful part of the literature review in that it allows you to speculate or theorise about things that were unexpected, surprising and challenging. It also allows you to honestly address some of the inevitable limitations that arise from any literature review, including the most thorough of systematic reviews.

Table 8.5 provides some issues and prompt questions to get you actively thinking about what you should aim to address in your discussion section.

Table 8.5   Some prompt questions for your discussion section

Issue	Associated questions
Identifying gaps	Is there a significant gap or oversight in the current research literature that you can identify? If there are gaps, why do you think those gaps exist?
Scope of published research	Has the published research tended to focus on one particular group of people, environment or setting to the exclusion of others? If so, how is this likely to have shaped, influenced or biased the current literature?
Implications for research/practice	Does your literature review suggest that it would be useful for the research to move in a certain direction or change some aspect of its focus? What kinds of factors have influenced this? Does it seem as if the 'standard' way of doing research in this area is likely to change?
Limitations	What were the limitations of the review in terms of the design, methodology and focus? How did these constrain the review and how do they influence the findings? What factors have impacted on what it is possible to conclude from the literature review?
Complexity	Is there a sense that there may be greater complexity to talking about the particular subject than was originally expected? If so, what kinds of things contribute to this complex picture?

Conclusion

The concluding section for your literature review serves the same purpose as a conclusion in a standard essay or assignment. In it you should revisit the aims and objectives of the literature review and, in that context, restate the main findings and/or results. Your conclusion should emphasise your literature review's contribution to knowledge or understanding. However, this does not mean making 'grand claims' that cannot be supported – most contributions to knowledge are quite modest in scale.

The primary focus of your conclusion is on the implications of your findings. You may conclude that there are different implications for different stakeholder groups such as service users, carers, practitioners and academic researchers. In discussing implications, it may be useful to refer back to issues that were addressed in the discussion section, as it is likely that any limitations discussed there will be relevant. Remember that conclusions will only seem valid if they are consistent with, and supported by, the evidence that you have presented. Statements based on how you think things 'should be' will simply come across as being unsubstantiated personal opinion.

You should not be introducing new subject matter into your conclusion – the cardinal rule is that if something is important enough to mention, then it should have a place in the main part of your literature review. The conclusion helps the reader to understand the significance of your literature review findings, and this is particularly important when attempting to evaluate the effectiveness of practice interventions.

References and bibliography

It is vitally important that you include a full, complete reference list at the end of your literature review. Remember that your reference list will provide a very obvious indication of how wide your background reading has been. It's worth taking the time to ensure that all of your references and citations are complete and accurate. If you take a sloppy approach, consider what this is likely to imply about the thoroughness and quality of other parts of your literature review!

We will consider referencing skills in much greater detail in Chapter 9, which also provides some referencing exercises for you to practise your skills.

Developing a Critical Writing Style

We discussed ways of developing your critical and analytical skills in a broad sense in Chapter 6, but it's worth briefly thinking more specifically about how you demonstrate these aspects of your work in your writing. The process of writing critically requires an *active* engagement with the subject matter, which is very different from simply providing a descriptive account. A great method of learning more about critical writing techniques is to read the peer-reviewed work of others.

Take it apart to see how it works!

ACTIVITY

Time suggested: 30–45 minutes

For this activity take an academic article that you have already read (e.g. the one you used for 'The art of abstraction' activity), or that you are interested in reading. Read the article through once, fairly quickly, to get the general gist of what the author is writing about. Then go through and read the article again in more detail. Now answer the following questions:

- What kind of critical vocabulary do they use? Which words indicate to you that the author is presenting a critical point or comment?
- How do they structure their arguments?
- How do they go about comparing and contrasting things?
- To what extent do they appear to agree or disagree with the material they are considering, and how do they make this clear to the reader?
- How do they make use of evidence to support a particular argument or viewpoint?

Getting Stuck with Your Writing

It is inevitable that there will be occasions where you feel that you don't know what to write or you seem to have ground to a halt. This sense of 'being blocked' is a natural part of the writing process and affects even the most experienced of writers at times. The following tool encourages you to be clear about, and then face, the kinds of fears, anxieties and blockages that everybody encounters occasionally.

Acknowledging these fears and negative emotions can help you to move forward with a greater degree of clarity and confidence.

'Blasting through blocks' (Cameron, 1995)

Take a piece of paper, a page in your research journal or a new page on your word processer and:

1. List any frustrations you have in connection with your literature review – it doesn't matter how silly these might sound!
2. List any fears or anxieties you might have in connection with this piece of work.
3. Now ask yourself: 'Is that all? Have I got everything down on the page?' If anything else occurs to you, note it down.
4. Ask yourself: 'What have I got to gain by avoiding doing this piece of work?' Often, there will be some hidden pay-offs.
5. Now simply allow yourself to get on and write without fear. It doesn't have to be perfect first time. In fact, aim to get down a basic set of points and ideas with the knowledge that an early start gives you plenty of time to go back and revise things later.

NB: Julia Cameron's 'Blasting through Blocks' technique is described in more detail in her book on creativity, called *The Artist's Way* (Cameron, 1995: 158).

The 'small chunks' technique

The aim of the 'small chunks' technique is to take the 'fear factor' out of the very idea of having to write something as complex and in-depth as a literature review. It's based on the idea that if you fixate on everything you need to do to get to the end of a project, you can convince yourself that you'll never get there! Sound familiar? Breaking mammoth tasks down into smaller parts makes them seem much more approachable and 'do-able'.

To use this approach:

- Make a list of the separate tasks, sections, parts or different activities that contribute towards the end goal, i.e. writing the literature review.
- Make a start somewhere on your list – whichever list item feels easiest to begin with – and, when finished, move on to the next item.
- If you get stuck, move on to another list item and come back when you feel ready.
- Keep an eye on your overall progress so you don't lose track of the bigger picture.

Editing, Redrafting and Proofreading

Editing, redrafting and proofreading are more than simply 'good things to do if you can make the time for them'. They are a key part of writing the kind of *adequate* and *appropriate* literature review we discussed earlier. Figure 8.1 gives you an idea of why you need to check your work carefully.

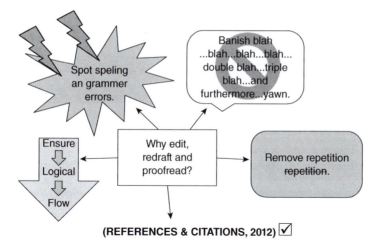

Figure 8.1   Why you need to edit, redraft and proofread your review

Editing and redrafting gives you the opportunity to amend or change anything that you are not happy with before you submit your literature review for assessment or peer-review (in the case of writing for publication). Even professional writers rarely get it right the first time and may need to produce any number of drafts until they are satisfied with what they have written. So:

- ensure you allow sufficient time to edit and redraft your work
- be prepared to be critical and analytical about your own work
- save each substantially different draft as a separate, numbered document so that you can always go back to an earlier version if necessary.

It can be notoriously difficult to proofread your own work, as we tend to make the same kinds of errors habitually and therefore become unaware that we are making them.

Think about... Mind the gap!

When reading our work through, our brains have a tendency to 'fill in' gaps according to what we expect to read rather than what we actually read. As an exaggerated example of this, read the following sentence which became a popular internet meme a few years ago:

Arocdnicg to rsceearch at Cmabrigde Uinervtisy, it deosn't mttaer in waht oredr the ltteers in a wrod are, the olny iprmoatnt tihng is taht the frist and lsat ltteer are in the rghit pcale. The rset can be a toatl mses and you can sitll raed it wouthit pobelrm. Tihs is buseace the huamn mnid deos not raed ervey lteter by istlef, but the wrod as a wlohe.

Although the letters are jumbled we can still make sense of the sentence. (As a side-note, there is no evidence that Cambridge University carried out such research – another reminder not to believe everything you receive in an email!)

The following tips can be useful for making your proofreading more effective:

- Find a way of focusing on each individual word, either by reading it out loud, experimenting with the speed at which you read, pointing to each individual word, and so on.
- Make a list of the things you repeatedly make errors on, and pay particular attention to checking these when you proofread.
- Ask someone else to read through your work to see if they pick up anything that you don't spot, and if there's anything that crops up more than once add it to your list of things to check in future.
- Don't rely too heavily on automated spelling and grammar checking – they help you to pick some things up but are not capable of flagging up all issues.

QUICK TIP: Proofread with different critical lenses!

As an alternative to trying to do all of the important work involved in proofreading in one read-through of your text, try out the following approach and see how it works for you:

- Proofread the work for spelling and grammar errors only.
- Proofread again but this time focus on checking the accuracy of citations and references only.
- Proofread a third time and focus only on checking that ideas are clearly expressed in a logical way.

Although this approach sounds like it will create more work for you, it can be a more effective and efficient way of checking all of the different aspects of your writing, as you are not having to apply several different critical lenses all at once.

Criticism as a Tool for Writing Development

Whether you are writing a literature review for an academic assignment or for publication, at some stage you may be offered criticism and feedback on draft or even final versions of your work. In academic publishing it is usual for writing to go through a peer-review process, in which subject experts offer feedback and constructive criticism on the work. Academic courses should incorporate several opportunities for you to receive detailed feedback on the quality of your writing, including specific guidance about how you could improve it.

Try to approach any constructive criticism you are offered with an open mind, and think about how the suggestions given could be used to make your work more effective. It is often difficult to receive criticism, as typically we like to feel like we have done a good job and it can feel deflating and demoralising to be told that there are areas of our work that could be further improved. However, try to resist the trap of taking criticism too personally, but instead see if you can view it as a tool to help you become even more effective in the future. One simple way of putting this into action is to ask yourself three simple questions:

1. *What* is this feedback telling me about my writing?
2. *What* could I now do differently?
3. *How* will I ensure I do this next time I write?

Ideas for Taking Things Further

1   When you next complete some written work on your literature review, try the 'proofreading with different critical lenses' approach outlined earlier in the chapter. Do you find it helps to focus on different issues with each reading?
2   Find a literature review which relates to a social care topic. Read it through and pay particular attention to the role and function that each section of the review performs. Make notes (either on a printed copy or add electronic 'comments' to a PDF or word-processed document) about what these roles and functions are. By 'reverse engineering' it in this way, you should come to a better appreciation of how it works as a literature review, giving you a sense of what you will need to seek to address in your own literature review writing.
3   *SCIE Systematic Research Reviews: Guidelines* (2nd edition) (Rutter et al., 2010) includes a section on reporting research reviews (pp. 65–77). Read this to gain an insight into the writing challenges for those preparing professional systematic reviews. You can also access this document at: www.scie.org.uk/publications/researchresources/rr01.pdf

Chapter Summary

• We have considered some of the important planning and preparation issues that you need to think about before beginning the process of writing.
• We have considered the role of describing, explaining and justifying in the writing of literature reviews (Hart, 1998).
• We have provided an overview of the sections you would expect to find in a typical literature review, and have considered some of the differing challenges involved in writing them.
• We have identified some tools and techniques that you could try to help you with various aspects of the writing process, including planning, structuring, proofreading and dealing with writer's block.

Further Reading and Useful Resources

Aveyard, H. (2007) *Doing a Literature Review in Health and Social Care*. Maidenhead: Open University Press. (Chapters 5, 6, 7 and 8 all include sections on writing aspects of the literature review.)

Hargreaves, S. (ed.) (2007) *Study Skills for Dyslexic Students*. London: Sage. (Chapter 6, 'Structuring different writing genres', by Helen Birkmyre, contains sections on writing abstracts and literature reviews and is especially written to help support students with dyslexia.)

Ridley, D. (2008) *The Literature Review: A Step-by-Step Guide for Students*. London: Sage. (Chapter 9, 'Foregrounding writer voice', provides some useful ideas and practical strategies for exploring your own writer voice in the context of writing a literature review.)

Stogdon, C. and Kiteley, R. (2010) *Study Skills for Social Workers*. Sage Study Skills Series. London: Sage. (See especially Chapter 7, 'Writing effectively'.)

Companion for Undergraduate Dissertations: Sociology, Anthropology, Politics, Social Policy, Social Work and Criminology [Online]. Available at: www.socscidiss.bham.ac.uk/ (accessed 6 March 2011). (This useful website is more generally focused on the broad area of undergraduate dissertation writing in the social sciences, but does include specific sections on developing and writing literature reviews.)

References

Cameron, J. (1995) *The Artist's Way*. London: Pan Macmillan.

Carnwell, R. and Daly, W. (2001) 'Strategies for the construction of a critical review of the literature', *Nurse Education in Practice*, 1(2): 57–63.

Cronin, P., Ryan, F. and Coughlan, M. (2008) 'Undertaking a literature review: a step-by-step approach', *British Journal of Nursing*, 17(1): 38–43.

Hart, C. (1998) *Doing a Literature Review*. London: Sage.

Rutter, D., Francis, J., Coren, E. and Fisher, M. (2010) *SCIE Systematic Research Reviews: Guidelines* (2nd edition). London: Social Care Institute for Excellence.

Wiles, R., Heath, S., Crow, G. and Charles, V. (2005) *Informed Consent in Social Research: A Literature Review*. ESRC National Centre for Research Methods [Online]. Available at: http://eprints.ncrm.ac.uk/85/1/MethodsReviewPaperNCRM-001.pdf (accessed 17 February 2012).

9

Referencing Skills

☑ Learning Outcomes ☑

- To develop your understanding of what referencing is and why it is important to get it right when working on literature reviews
- To develop your awareness of plagiarism and the role that referencing has in relation to good academic practices
- To develop your understanding of how to reference in different contexts and using different types of material, using real examples
- To develop your awareness of referencing management software, such as EndNote and Zotero, and the role of plagiarism detection software

What is Referencing?

Referencing is simply a way of indicating exactly where you have taken your information from. Such information will typically include:

- ideas
- statistics
- quotes
- models
- theories
- concepts
- other types of information you have come across.

When drawing on this material, you must indicate what the original source of this information is, so that the reader is clear about its derivation.

? Did you know? Referencing systems ?

There are many different types of referencing system and some subject areas may favour particular approaches to referencing. However, the author–date system (which includes Harvard and APA styles) is widely used within British higher education institutions (Neville, 2010: 47–48) and is the one that we will focus on in this chapter. If you are preparing work for an academic course, it is absolutely essential that you check with your course tutors as to which referencing style should be used, as many institutions do vary in the way in which they require references to be formulated, presented and punctuated. All institutions should provide clear referencing guidance containing examples of citation and referencing for a range of sources. Alternatively, if you are preparing something for publication, then check with your publisher as to which system should be used. If you are required to use a system that is different from the 'author–date' one (e.g. numerical), please refer to the books listed at the end of this chapter for further guidance.

Why Do I Need to Reference?

If it helps, you could think about the similarities between writing an essay (assignment or literature review) and presenting a case in a court of law.

Think about it... Essays/assignments vs court cases

If you tried to present a case in a court of law without providing any evidence of the truthfulness or reliability of your claims, it is highly unlikely that the Judge would find in your favour. Similarly, in an essay or assignment you are aiming to convince the reader of the truthfulness and reliability of your claims. You can only successfully do this by backing up your claims with valid and reliable evidence. Failing to provide any evidence, or basing claims on incomplete, weak or unattributed evidence, is only likely to undermine your case!

Correct citation and referencing is important in all pieces of academic work, but is absolutely essential in literature reviews, as the whole point of writing a literature review is to provide an accurate account of the literature.

ACTIVITY

The importance of evidence and attribution

Time suggested: 3–5 minutes

Read through the brief excerpts from two different introductions to the same issue, shown below. One is the direct text from a genuine journal article (Hill and Brettle, 2006), and the other is a paraphrased summary.

1. Which version is most informative?
2. Which version would you trust the most, and why?
3. Which version demonstrates evidence of wider reading?

Introduction (Version A)

It is a well-established fact that the UK has an ageing population, and that this trend will continue to increase as we move further into the millennium. The increase in health problems that age brings has meant that the government has had to take this issue more seriously, and the increased amount of money that the government has put into services for older people over recent years is evidence of this. However, money alone is not enough to address the increased need, and so extra professionals have been recruited to address the particular needs of older people.

Introduction (Version B)

The ageing of the UK population is well documented, with the number of people over the age of 80 projected to increase by almost a half and the number of people over 90 to double by 2025 (Department of Health, 2001). As certain health problems increase with age, the government has established a National Service Framework for older people and committed an extra £1.4 billion to expanding health and social care services for older people. This includes an extra 2,500 therapists and other professionals to provide person-centred care, which meets individual needs, supports independence and sustains older people within the community (Department of Health, 2001).

Plagiarism

What is plagiarism?

In the context of higher education, 'plagiarism' refers to a number of situations where a student is considered to have cheated by using the work of others and passing this off as their own original work.

Spot the plagiarist!

Time suggested: 2 minutes

Read through the following statements, and select 'Yes' if you think the student has been guilty of plagiarism, or 'No' if you think they have not:

A. Maria did not do much background reading for her literature review and was struggling to find enough to write about. She asked her friend, Gemma, if she could borrow her literature review for 'ideas', and ended up copying five paragraphs word for word. Yes / No

B. Gemma lent her literature review to her friend, Maria, who was struggling to come up with ideas of what to write about for her own work. Yes / No

ACTIVITY

(Continued)

(Continued)

C. Paul was not at all confident about the topic of his assignment, so was delighted when he found a website which seemed to contain all of the information he needed. He knew he shouldn't copy and paste this information so instead he put it all into his own words. As he wasn't using direct quotes he didn't feel there was a need to include a reference to the website. Yes / No

---

Answer: Cases A and C would be clear examples of students plagiarising the work of others. Although Gemma didn't attempt to plagiarise in example B, she would still find herself in trouble for collusion, and may be part of the plagiarism investigation into Maria's work. Although you may feel that you are being helpful by offering to show others your work, the truth is that you never know how it will be used. This is why you should never pass on your work to others.

?   Did you know? Electronic plagiarism detection software   ?

Many academic institutions require students to submit their work electronically these days, and as part of this process they may use an electronic plagiarism detection service. This is a massive database which compares your work against much of the content on the World Wide Web, as well as previous submissions by students at institutions across the whole country. So, your tutor can tell at a glance if a large proportion of what you have written has come from elsewhere. Of course, if you have used some direct quotes in your work, this is perfectly acceptable as long as you have indicated that these were taken from other sources by providing a citation and reference. However, if you have copied and pasted material from other places which you haven't acknowledged properly in your work, this may lead to significantly reduced marks, failure of the assignment and the possibility of being required to attend a plagiarism investigation panel.

When Do I Need to Reference?

The main situations in which you need to provide a citation and reference are:

- when you are using a direct quote from a published source
- when you are paraphrasing (i.e. putting into your own words) something you have read about elsewhere
- when you are drawing on any kind of information from another source to support your work (e.g. statistics, examples, cases, trends, etc.)
- when using ideas or theories that others have developed (e.g. attachment theory, Thompson's PCS Model, social and medical models of disability).

When Don't I Need to Provide a Reference?

You do not need to provide a reference when you are writing about a fact that is considered to be in the general public domain. For instance, if I write that currently

David Cameron is the Prime Minister of the UK, I don't need to supply a citation and reference because this is a fact that can be considered to be widely known.

ACTIVITY

References required?

Read through the following list of scenarios. Your task is to decide whether the student needs to include a reference (☑) in their work or not (☒).

1. Mohammed uses a definition of the term 'evidence-based practice' which he takes from a dictionary of social work terms.
2. Penny writes a paragraph explaining the main differences between qualitative and quantitative research.
3. Justin writes that 8,700 young people between the ages of 10 and 15 were subject to a child protection plan between 2008 and 2009.
4. Ellie uses a direct quotation in her introduction.
5. Ben borrows the rough work of a colleague, Natalie, and uses this as the basis on which to write his own work. He summarises many of the points that Natalie makes, but doesn't use any direct quotes.
6. Saira recalls some research findings reported by a lecturer in a recent lecture session. She summarises these in her discussion section.
7. Vicky writes that the body that regulates the social work profession in the UK is known as the Health and Care Professions Council.

How Do I Reference Correctly?

References are made up of two parts:

1. The first part of a reference is called a **citation** (which is a fancy name for a short reference). Citations appear in the main part of your literature review, essay or assignment.
2. The second part of your reference is called the **full reference**, which goes in the reference list that should appear at the end of your piece of work (after your conclusion). Your reference list should be presented in alphabetical order (see the reference list for this chapter on page 139 for an example).

> **?   Did you know? Why is a reference made up of two parts?   ?**
>
> If we put the full reference details of every source that we've used in the main body of our work, we would be making our readers do a lot of unnecessary reading and they'd probably soon get bored and frustrated.

Citations

So, instead of having to put the full reference in our work every time we refer to a source, we use a shortened version instead, which is known as a citation.

In author–date referencing systems the citation is just made up of (1) the author's surname, (2) the year the source was published and (3) a page number if you are using a direct quote, or paraphrasing a specific point or section of the text. So, an example would be: 'The more you use your referencing skills, the more accomplished you will become at producing academic references' (Stogdon and Kiteley, 2010: 121). This is much shorter and easier to read than a full reference! Of course, you still need to record the full reference details for the source you are using, but these appear in the reference list at the end of your work.

There are some exceptions where citations may vary slightly. For instance:

- If there is no author's name, use the name of the organisation that has published the website, e.g. MIND, SCOPE, Kirklees Social Services, etc.
- If there is no date of publication available, use the words (no date) or the abbreviation (n.d.) where you would normally put the year.

The following pages look in detail at how you would go about putting together the citations and full references for a range of information sources that you are likely to encounter. We have used Pears and Shields' guidance on Harvard referencing in the book, *Cite Them Right* (2010), as the model for these illustrative examples, as this is a popular referencing resource for UK higher education. However, be aware that there may be differences in the ways in which other institutions or publishers (if writing for publication) require you to reference in your work, and familiarise yourself with these from the outset. Nonetheless, the following general principles will apply across most author–date referencing systems.

Full References

Referencing a book

The information required to reference a book is given in Table 9.1.

Table 9.1

Author's surname(s) followed by initials	Year of publication in brackets	Title of book in italics	Place book was published	Publishing company which published book
Stogdon, C. and Kiteley, R.	(2010)	*Study Skills for Social Workers*	London:	Sage

So, an example **citation** for this source would be:

... the significance of service-user feedback is highlighted by Stogdon and Kiteley (2010: 170).

The **full reference** would be:

Stogdon, C. and Kiteley, R. (2010) *Study Skills for Social Workers*. London: Sage.

If you are unsure about where to find all of these pieces of information, the cover and publishing details page for the example in Table 9.1 has been included below (see Figure 9.1). It clearly identifies where each piece of information that makes up the reference can be found.

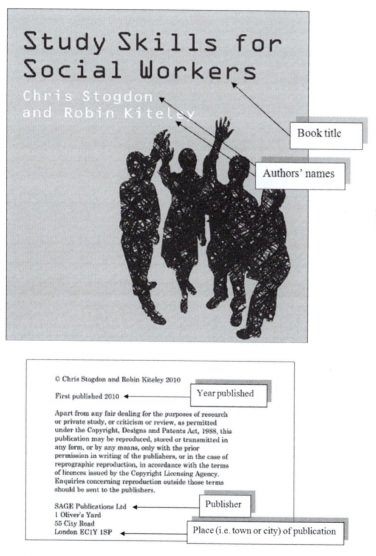

Figure 9.1   Where to find reference information from a book cover and copyright page

NOTE: Publishing information is usually shown one or two pages into the book, often on the reverse side of the second page.

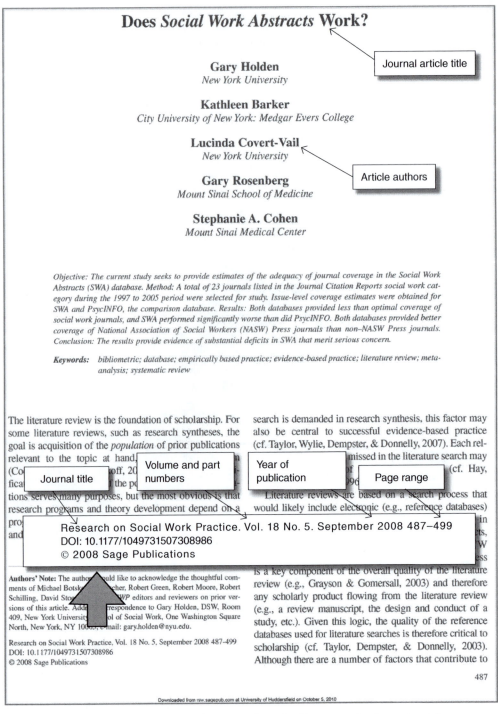

Figure 9.2   Where to find reference information from the first page of a journal article

Referencing a journal article

The information required to reference a journal article is given in Table 9.2.

Table 9.2

Author's surname(s) followed by initials	Year of publication in brackets	Article title in single quotation marks	Journal title in italics	Volume and issue or part number	Page range of article
Holden, G., Barker, K., Covert-Vail, L., Rosenberg, G. and Cohen, S.A.	(2008)	'Does Social Work Abstracts Work?'	*Research on Social Work Practice*	Vol. 18, No. 5	pp. 487–499

So, an example **citation** for this source would be:

... Holden et al. (2008, p.490) carried out a longitudinal study in their examination of the adequacy of journal coverage in Social Work Abstracts.

The **full reference** would be:

Holden, G., Barker, K., Covert-Vail, L., Rosenberg, G. and Cohen, S.A. (2008) 'Does Social Work Abstracts Work?', *Research on Social work Practice*, 18(5), p.487–499.

Referencing a web page

The information required to reference a web page is given in Table 9.3.

Table 9.3

Author's surname(s) followed by initials or name or organisation that published website	Year of publication in brackets or (no date)	Title of web page in italics	Available at: web address	(Accessed day, month, year)
Social Care Institute for Excellence	(no date)	*Adult Safeguarding*	Available at: www.scie.org.uk/ adults/ safeguarding/ index.asp	(Accessed 31 May 2011)

So, an example citation for this source would be:

... safeguarding involves three core elements (Social Care Institute for Excellence, no date).

The **full reference** would be:

Social Care Institute for Excellence (no date) *Adult Safeguarding*. Available at: www.scie.org.uk/adults/safeguarding/index.asp (Accessed 31 May 2011).

The screenshot in Figure 9.3 shows the actual web page that this example refers to, and indicates where the information that makes up the full reference can be found.

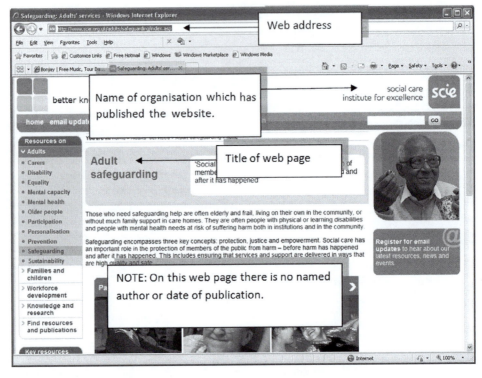

Figure 9.3   Where to find reference information from a web page

Used with permission from Social Care Institute for Excellence

Referencing an electronic book

The information required to reference an electronic book (eBook) is given in Table 9.4.

So, an example **citation** for this source would be:

Table 9.4

Author's surname(s) followed by initials	Year of publication in brackets	eBook title in italics	Name of eBook provider or collection in italics, followed by [Online]	Available at: web address.	(Accessed: day, month, year)
Ferguson, I.	(2008)	*Reclaiming Social Work: Challenging Neo-liberalism and Promoting Social Justice*	Ebrary [Online]	Available at: http://site.ebrary. com/lib/uoh/ docDetail. action?docID= 10285211&force=1	(Accessed: 15 May 2011)

... the hope that may arise from resistance to managerialism within social work has been explored by Ferguson (2008).

The **full reference** would be:

Ferguson, I. (2008) *Reclaiming Social Work: Challenging Neo-liberalism and Promoting Social Justice. Ebrary* [Online]. Available at: http://site.ebrary.com/lib/uoh/docDetail. action?docID=10285211&force=1 (Accessed: 15 May 2011).

The screenshot in Figure 9.4 shows an eBook being viewed using the Ebrary electronic book service and indicates where the information that makes up the

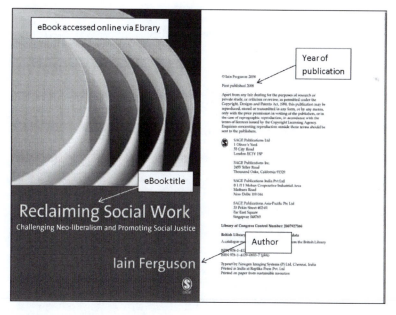

Figure 9.4   Where to find the reference information from an eBook using the Ebrary electronic book service

full reference can be found. (*Note*: Your institution may subscribe to Ebrary or other eBook providers. If you are unsure, ask your tutors or a member of your library staff.)

Referencing an electronic journal article

The information required to reference an electronic journal article is given in Table 9.5.

Table 9.5

Author's surname(s) followed by initials	Year of publication in brackets	Title of journal article in single quotation marks	Title of journal in italics	Volume and issue or part number	Page range
Hamilton, K.	(2009)	'Low-income families: experiences and responses to consumer exclusion'	*International Journal of Sociology and Social Policy*	Vol. 29, No. 9/10	pp. 543–557

Name of database provider in italics, followed by [Online]	Available at: web address of database provider	(Accessed day, month and year)
Emerald Insight [Online].	Available at: www. emeraldinsight.com/0144-333X.htm	(Accessed 28 May 2011)

So, an example **citation** for this source would be:

... Hamilton (2009) discusses the stigma management techniques that excluded consumers may use.

The **full reference** would be:

Hamilton, K. (2009) 'Low-income families: experiences and responses to consumer exclusion', *International Journal of Sociology and Social Policy*, 29(9/10): 543–557, *Emerald Insight* [Online]. Available at: www.emeraldinsight.com/0144-333X.htm (Accessed 28 May 2011).

Figure 9.5 shows the first page of a journal article that was accessed electronically. The labels and arrows show where some of the relevant information required for the full reference can be found.

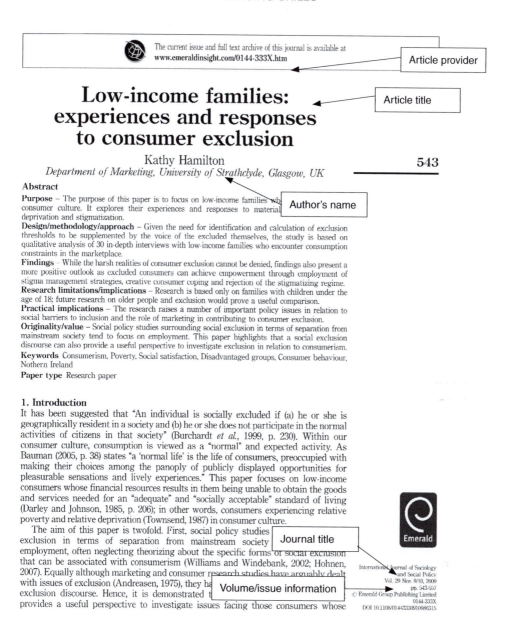

Article provider

Low-income families: experiences and responses to consumer exclusion

Article title

Kathy Hamilton

543

Department of Marketing, University of Strathclyde, Glasgow, UK

Author's name

Abstract

Purpose – The purpose of this paper is to focus on low-income families who consumer culture. It explores their experiences and responses to material deprivation and stigmatization.

Design/methodology/approach – Given the need for identification and calculation of exclusion thresholds to be supplemented by the voice of the excluded themselves, the study is based on qualitative analysis of 30 in-depth interviews with low-income families who encounter consumption constraints in the marketplace.

Findings – While the harsh realities of consumer exclusion cannot be denied, findings also present a more positive outlook as excluded consumers can achieve empowerment through employment of stigma management strategies, creative consumer coping and rejection of the stigmatizing regime.

Research limitations/implications – Research is based only on families with children under the age of 18; future research on older people and exclusion would prove a useful comparison.

Practical implications – The research raises a number of important policy issues in relation to social barriers to inclusion and the role of marketing in contributing to consumer exclusion.

Originality/value – Social policy studies surrounding social exclusion in terms of separation from mainstream society tend to focus on employment. This paper highlights that a social exclusion discourse can also provide a useful perspective to investigate exclusion in relation to consumerism.

Keywords Consumerism, Poverty, Social satisfaction, Disadvantaged groups, Consumer behaviour, Nothern Ireland

Paper type Research paper

1. Introduction

It has been suggested that "An individual is socially excluded if (a) he or she is geographically resident in a society and (b) he or she does not participate in the normal activities of citizens in that society" (Burchardt *et al*, 1999, p. 230). Within our consumer culture, consumption is viewed as a "normal" and expected activity. As Bauman (2005, p. 38) states "a 'normal life' is the life of consumers, preoccupied with making their choices among the panoply of publicly displayed opportunities for pleasurable sensations and lively experiences." This paper focuses on low-income consumers whose financial resources results in them being unable to obtain the goods and services needed for an "adequate" and "socially acceptable" standard of living (Darley and Johnson, 1985, p. 206); in other words, consumers experiencing relative poverty and relative deprivation (Townsend, 1987) in consumer culture.

The aim of this paper is twofold. First, social policy studies exclusion in terms of separation from mainstream society ̄ employment, often neglecting theorizing about the specific forms of social exclusion that can be associated with consumerism (Williams and Windebank, 2002; Hohnen, 2007). Equally although marketing and consumer research studies have arguably dealt with issues of exclusion (Andreasen, 1975), they ha exclusion discourse. Hence, it is demonstrated t provides a useful perspective to investigate issues facing those consumers whose

Journal title

Emerald

Volume/issue information

International Journal of Sociology and Social Policy
Vol. 29 Nos. 9/10, 2009
pp. 543-557
© Emerald Group Publishing Limited
0144-333X
DOI 10.1108/01443330910986315

Figure 9.5 Where to find the reference information from a journal article that has been accessed electronically

Referencing a book chapter (from an edited collection)

The information required to reference a book chapter from an edited collection is given in Table 9.6.

Table 9.6

Chapter author's surname(s) followed by initials	Year of publication in brackets	Title of chapter in single quotation marks	in: Book editor surname(s)followed by initials and 'ed.' or 'eds' if more than one
Hall, T.	(2001)	'Caught not taught: ethnographic research at a young people's accommodation project',	in: Shaw, I. and Gould, N. (eds)

Title of book in italics	Place book was published	Publishing company which published book	Page range (i.e. start page and end page) for chapter
Qualitative Research in Social Work	London	Sage	pp. 49–59.

So, an example **citation** for this source would be:

> ... Hall (2001) took an ethnographic approach to researching issues of social exclusion in relation to young, homeless people.

The **full reference** would be:

Hall, T. (2001) 'Caught not taught: ethnographic research at a young people's accommodation project', in Shaw, I. and Gould, N. (eds) *Qualitative Research in Social Work*. London: Sage, pp. 49–59.

Figure 9.6 shows the book cover and the first page of a chapter from a book which contains a series of chapters by different authors. The labels and arrows show where the information required for the reference can be found.

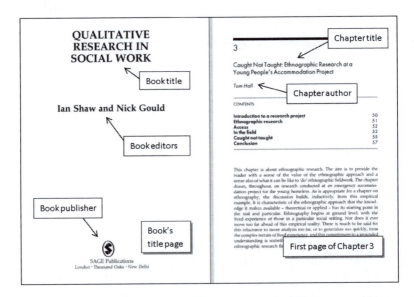

Figure 9.6   Where to find the reference information from a book chapter within an edited collection

Referencing government/official publications

The information required to reference government or official publications is given in Table 9.7.

Table 9.7

Country	Government department or organisation for which the publication has been produced	Year of publication in brackets	Title of publication in italics	Place publication was published	Publishing company which published the publication	Publication reference number in brackets (if available)
Great Britain	Department for Education	(2011)	*Letting Children be Children*	London:	The Stationery Office	(CM 8078)

So, an example **citation** for this source would be:

... issues relating to the commercialisation, and in particular, sexualisation of childhood have been of recent concern (Great Britain. Department for Education, 2011).

The **full reference** would be:

Great Britain. Department for Education (2011) *Letting Children be Children*. London: The Stationery Office (Cm. 8078).

Figure 9.7 shows the document that this example reference was taken from, and the labels and arrows show where to find the relevant information required for the full reference.

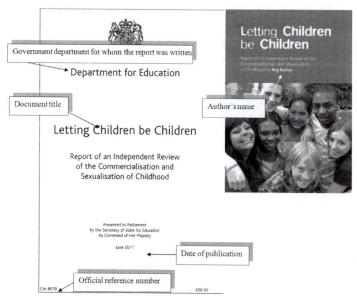

Figure 9.7   Where to find the reference information from government or official publications

Referencing an Act of Parliament

When writing about social work issues you will often need to refer to the relevant pieces of legislation that guide your practice and that shape and influence the way social policy develops.

The information required to reference an Act of Parliament is given in Table 9.8.

Table 9.8

Country	Title of Act, including year, in italics	Name of sovereign and chapter number of the Act in italics	Year of publication in round brackets	Place Act was published	Publisher of the Act
Great Britain	*Health and Social Care Act 2008*	*Elizabeth II. c.14*	(2008)	London:	The Stationery Office

So, an example **citation** for this source would be:

... as a result of changes to the legal context (Great Britain. *Health and Social Care Act 2008*).

The **full reference** would be:

Great Britain. *Health and Social Care Act 2008: Elizabeth II. c.14* (2008) London: The Stationery Office.

Figure 9.8 shows the first page of the *Health and Social Care Act 2008* to give you an idea of the kind of format that is used for these documents. The labels and arrows show you where the key information required for a full reference can be found.

Reference Management Software

It is a really good idea to practise referencing without the aid of computer programs because:

- you will get a better understanding of how citation and referencing works
- you will become more attuned to the kinds of information that you need to be looking out for as you conduct your reading
- software doesn't always behave in the way that we expect (due to different options and settings, etc.).

However, it is useful to be aware that there are several software programs that can help you with the process of recording information and producing your final

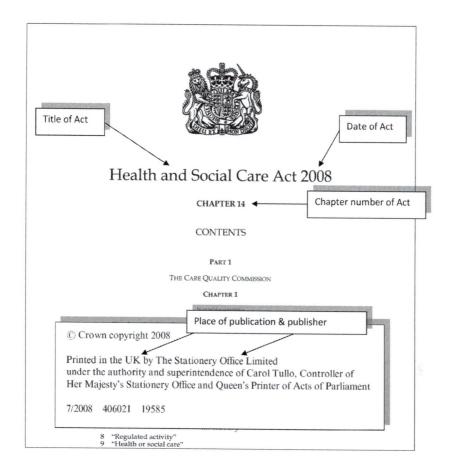

Figure 9.8   Where to find the reference information from an Act of Parliament

reference list. Your institution or employer may already provide access to a commercial referencing package, such as EndNote, or you may choose to explore the range of free software packages that can be downloaded from the web.

?   Did you know? Software which helps with referencing   ?

This box provides a brief summary of some of the more popular referencing packages that are available:

EndNote is a flexible package that enables users to:

(Continued)

(Continued)

- record their referencing information in one convenient place
- input a whole range of different reference types (e.g. from books to DVDs)
- use different referencing styles (Harvard, Vancouver, APA, and so on)
- store different kinds of documents including Word documents and PDF files, so it can be used as a library to keep all of their important research documents together
- insert full references into their Word document quickly and easily, in the desired format (e.g. Harvard), using an installable feature called Cite While You Write™.

Ask your institution or employer if they make EndNote available, and also if they have any training materials, courses or workshops which can help you to learn how to use it effectively.

Zotero is an example of a free, open source referencing program. 'Open source' means that it is developed by a group of volunteer programmers who all work together to develop and upgrade the program rather than it being developed by a commercial organisation. For this reason, open source software is often free to download and install on your computer. Zotero enables users to:

- record and manage a range of different reference types
- manage a range of document types, including PDF documents, which means that you can use it to keep track of your documents
- use it in conjunction with Microsoft Word or OpenOffice to generate in-text citations and full reference lists.

There are many other referencing management software programs available, and some are open source and free to use. We do not endorse any particular product but would refer interested readers to software comparison web pages such as http://en.wikipedia.org/wiki/Comparison_of_reference_management_software

Think about it… Referencing rage and steps to avoid it!

Although referencing is a fairly straightforward process, there are a number of common things that can go wrong:

- Not doing enough background reading – it doesn't matter how good your referencing skills are if you haven't actually done enough reading around your subject. If you've only read two books, you will only have two references! A reader can instantly get a sense of how much reading you are likely to have done before they even read your work, by simply looking at your reference list.

TAKE ACTION: In a literature review, the breadth and relevance of your reading is key to success so make sure you read as widely as possible.

- Not keeping records of what you've read – if you haven't kept a note of the relevant details of what you've been reading (e.g. title, author's name, journal article title, journal title, etc.), how are you going to be able to provide a full and accurate reference?

TAKE ACTION: Use a notebook, spreadsheet or reference management software to record relevant details of your sources, as you go along.

- Not realising when you should be using citation and referencing – if you are drawing on the work of others to support the points you make in your academic work but don't acknowledge this, you are in danger of looking as though you have plagiarised (i.e. cheated).

TAKE ACTION: If you are not sure what constitutes plagiarism, check your institution's guidance on this. Remember, if in doubt – check it out!

- Not being consistent – the reason why some students find referencing a bit fiddly is that you are asked to present specific pieces of information in specific ways. What we often find is that students get this right some of the time but then make systematic errors in other cases.

TAKE ACTION: Use correct referencing examples to guide you when you reference and always give yourself enough time to carefully proofread your work before you submit it.

- Using an incorrect referencing system – there's nothing worse than spending ages getting all of your citation and referencing correct only to realise you've used the wrong system.

TAKE ACTION: Check which system is used by your academic institution or, if submitting to a journal, check their referencing requirements. In both cases this information will be available online.

Referencing Quirks

In this chapter we have provided examples of how to reference many of the common sources that you are likely to use in the course of writing a literature review, assignment or essay. However, there are some cases where things are not as straight forward and it helps to know some additional referencing 'conventions' (i.e. rules) to help with this. For instance:

- If you wanted to cite a journal article written by eight authors in your literature review, do you need to list the surnames of all eight authors every time you cite the article?
- What would you do if you wanted to write about a report which you have not read yourself but which was discussed in a journal article you have read?

The frequently asked questions (FAQs) in Table 9.9 give answers to these and other referencing queries.

Table 9.9   Frequently asked questions about referencing

Frequently asked questions	Answers and examples
1. My source was written by seven authors. Do I need to include all of their names in my citation?	No. If your source is written by three authors or more, you can normally list the first-named author and then use the abbreviation 'et al.' (which means 'and others'). Some specific referencing systems differ in how they implement this, so do check specific guidance for the system you are using. E.g. Gregory et al., 2007 NB: If your source was written by two authors, you would simply use both author surnames.
2. My source was written by seven authors. Do I need to include all of their names in my reference?	Yes. All of the author names must be shown in the full reference, but at least you only need to write the full reference once!
3. What should I do if there is no named author or date of publication?	We covered this earlier in the chapter, but to recap: • If there is no author name, use the name of the organisation that has published the work. • If there is no date, put the words no date or n.d. in the brackets instead. E.g. … as recently reported (SCIE, n.d.).
4. I need to cite three different works by the same author which were all published in 2003. If I just use the author's surname (e.g. Giddens) and the date (2003), how will the reader know which of the three different works I am referring to?	To differentiate several works that were produced by the same author in the same year, add a letter at the end of the year. E.g. Giddens (2003a) wrote that…, Giddens (2003b) argued that…, Giddens (2003c) proved that… Use the same letters to identify these sources in your full reference list.
5. I want to provide a citation and reference to a source (e.g. Harrison, 1999) that I haven't actually read, but that was mentioned in a book/journal that I did read (e.g. McGrath, 2006). What do I need to do?	In all cases, you would be best advised to try to get hold of the original piece of work itself (e.g. Harrison, 1999), so that you can draw your own conclusions about it, rather than rely on another author's (i.e. McGrath, 2006) interpretation. However, in some cases this may prove very difficult so you can use a method known as 'secondary referencing'. To do this, when citing the work you need to make it clear that you didn't read the original: e.g. … Harrison (1999, cited in McGrath, 2006) states that … When it comes to providing the full reference, you only use the details of the source that you actually read yourself (i.e. McGrath, 2006): McGrath, C. (2006) *Evidence based practice*. Edinburgh: Brilliant Books.
6. What should I do if I want to cite multiple sources to support an argument, observation or other type of comment?	Multiple sources are normally separated by the use of the semi-colon (;). Pears and Shields (2010: 5) indicate that multiple cited sources should be shown in chronological order, with the most recent sources appearing first. However, this can vary from system to system so check your specific referencing guidance. E.g. … this bias has been reported in numerous studies (Jenkins, 2013; Madeley, 2010; Shah, 2007).

What is missing?

Spot the referencing omissions! In this exercise you are asked to identify which pieces of information are missing.

Reference List

Brown, L. (2010) 'Balancing Risk and Innovation to Improve Social Work Practice' *British Journal of Social Work*.

Donald Schön. The Reflective Practitioner. Aldershot: Arena.

SCIE (online) www.scie.org.uk/topic/people/olderpeople

ACTIVITY

The importance of evidence and attribution

Hopefully, you will have concluded that Version B is the better version, for the following reasons:

1. It is more informative – it gives specific details, dates and figures.
2. It is most trustworthy – the sources of these details, dates and figures are clearly shown in the form of a correctly formatted citation.
3. It demonstrates evidence of reading – again the citations indicate this.

Version A demonstrates some knowledge and understanding but because we don't know from where the information is taken we can't even attempt to check it. More seriously, if you don't cite and reference your sources properly you may be suspected of plagiarism.

ANSWERS FOR ACTIVITY

References required?

1. Yes – he is using someone else's published definition of the term.
1. No, assuming she is drawing on her general knowledge of this.
2. Yes – where has Justin come across such specific statistical information?
3. Yes – she is using someone else's published words. (She also needs to remember to include a page number in her citation.)
4. Technically No – Ben cannot reference Natalie's work as such because it is unpublished. However, he should not be copying Natalie's work – this is collusion and both Ben and Natalie could end up in trouble for this.
5. Yes – there is a convention for citing and referencing lectures.
6. No – this can be considered to be general knowledge.

ANSWERS FOR ACTIVITY

ANSWERS FOR ACTIVITY

What is missing?

Reference List

Brown, L. (2010) 'Balancing Risk and Innovation to Improve Social Work Practice', *British Journal of Social Work*. VOLUME NUMBER, ISSUE NUMBER and PAGE RANGE missing.

Schön, D. (YEAR in brackets missing) *The Reflective Practitioner*. Aldershot: Arena. Also, the author's name was not correctly presented previously.

Social Care Institute for Excellence (DATE or N.D. missing) *TITLE OF WEB PAGE missing* AVAILABLE AT missing: www.scie.org.uk/topic/people/olderpeople. DATE ACCESSED missing.

Ideas for Taking Things Further

1. Digital media have provided many platforms for making information available and all of this can be formally referenced. Research how you would go about referencing:

    i. Podcasts
    ii. Wikis
    iii. Blogs
    iv. YouTube videos

2. PLATO is an online resource on academic referencing and contains tutorials, exercises and self-tests. Access the following brief 'attainment test' to see how well you have grasped the fundamentals of referencing: http://ucbonline.ucb.ac.uk/shared/plato/attain.html

3. Make some enquiries about whether your institution or employer provides access to any reference management software. If so, arrange for a quick demonstration (if possible) or find an online tutorial to help you get started.

Chapter Summary

- In this chapter we have considered what referencing is and why it is used in academic work.
- We have explained the difference between citations (short references), which go in the main body of your work, and full references, which go in a list at the end of your work.
- We have illustrated how to compose references for a number of different types of sources that you are likely to come across in reading for your literature review.
- We have discussed plagiarism and how it can be avoided by using effective citation and referencing.
- We have explored some of the options for using software programs to assist with the referencing process.
- We have outlined some of the quirks of referencing.

Further Reading and Useful Resources

Neville, C. (2010) *The Complete Guide to Referencing and Avoiding Plagiarism* (2nd edn). Maidenhead: Open University Press. (This book provides a detailed and in-depth overview of the referencing process. It explains how to use the different referencing styles that may be useful for those readers who need to use a style other than the Harvard System.)

Pears, R. and Shields, G. (2010) *Cite Them Right: The Essential Referencing Guide* (8th edn). Basingstoke: Palgrave Macmillan. (This is a very user-friendly guide to the referencing process, and proves to be popular with student readers.)

Stogdon, C. and Kiteley, R. (2010) *Study Skills for Social Workers*. Sage Study Skills Series. London: Sage. (See especially Chapter 8, 'Referencing effectively'. This chapter provides an overview of the referencing process and includes exercises and activities to encourage readers to practise their referencing skills.)

References

Hill, A. and Brettle, A. (2006) 'Counselling older people: what can we learn from the research evidence?' *Journal of Social Work Practice: Psychotherapeutic Approaches in Health, Welfare and the Community*, 20(3): 281–297.

Neville, C. (2010) *The Complete Guide to Referencing and Avoiding Plagiarism* (2nd edn). Maidenhead: Open University Press.

Pears, R. and Shields, G. (2010) *Cite Them Right: The Essential Referencing Guide* (8th edn). Basingstoke: Palgrave Macmillan.

Stogdon, C. and Kiteley, R. (2010) *Study Skills for Social Workers*. Sage Study Skills Series. London: Sage.

10

Evidence-based Practice

```
┌─────────────────────────────────────────────────────────────────┐
│                   ☑ Learning Outcomes ☑                          │
│                                                                   │
│  • To gain an overview of the range of academic literature in    │
│    evidence-based social work practice                           │
│  • To draw on the evidence to support professional judgements     │
│    and recommendations                                            │
│  • To be able to access appropriate evidence bases, e.g. CC Inform│
│  • To develop confidence in using academic sources                │
│  • To understand the role of evidence in producing robust reports │
│    in practice settings                                           │
└─────────────────────────────────────────────────────────────────┘
```

Why Evidence-based Practice?

As you undertake the preparations for your literature review, which will usually be a part of your own academic study, you may be wondering just why we are devoting time in this book to the discussion of evidence-based practice. Perhaps consider for a moment just why you have agreed to undertake a literature review? It may be that you have a specific area of social work theory that holds a particular interest for you and you want to explore this as part of your academic study? It may be that your course tutor has advised you to consider how you might use the subject of the literature review to inform areas of social work practice that you are currently involved with either academically, practically or both? If you are practising or planning to practise in a certain area, it may be that the subject of the literature review will be the base on which you will build your knowledge? For example, if you are applying for a post or being considered for a practice placement, you may need to look at current literature to inform your understanding of the specific area of practice and this initial exploration may then lead to a more formal review of the literature for an academic purpose.

You may not have noticed but the very fact that you have agreed (even if this has been under duress as the literature review is a mandatory part of your course work) to undertake a review of literature in your chosen area of social work means that you have engaged with the concepts of evidence-based practice. All theory and knowledge connect in some way to practice – discuss!

Looking at the evidence you already use

List some of your own experiences of applying knowledge or evidence to a practice setting. This may be in a practical way or through academic reading and writing essays.

If you have practised in social work, do you feel confident to explain to a service user the knowledge base that is informing your face-to-face work?

(This a tough question and we would suggest that not many very experienced social work practitioners would feel competent to explain their evidence base. We hope that through looking at the complexities of the knowledge/evidence that supports practice, you will begin to develop a confidence in your own practice.)

Defining Terms

At the outset, it is important to clarify the terms that we will use in this chapter to avoid confusion and misinterpretation. In this chapter we will highlight some of the key areas of the debates in evidence-based practice in social work and give you some direction to the relevant literature that you may find helpful in compiling your review.

We will not try to duplicate the current debates in evidence-based practice in social work as this has been done very successfully by others (e.g. Webb, 2006) and we have never subscribed to the reinvention of wheels! But we will offer you some guided references to some of the literature that supports the current themes in this area and that may have a relevance for you in the process of developing your own literature review. We do want to be clear about our connection of the concepts of knowledge and evidence, and although we are aware that some knowledge is informed by experience, we want to make the connection between knowledge as a base for evidence to support social work practice.

The term *evidence-based practice* is being used to describe social work practice that is informed by academically-tested knowledge and has credibility across social work disciplines.

In looking at the complexities of the knowledge base that informs evidence-based practice, it is also relevant to consider other factors. These factors include the public and political responses to social work tragedies that can assume a 'common sense' approach to social work practice. Webb critiques the concept of evidence-based practice that is based predominantly on the very traditional systems of the validation of knowledge and argues that the lack of recognition of the reflection that takes place in social work practice leaves a significant gap in establishing the relevant and informed evidence that will inform practice. Webb (2001) examined the background to evidence-based practice and looked at some of the key ideas and assumptions that have informed the debate. He argues that the attraction to a model of practice in social work that is based on clear and rigorous research-based evidence provides a potential panacea for the target-based and technocratic management culture that has been dominant in social work for the last two decades.

The attraction of a prescriptive 'theory and method' has the potential to appease the managerialists who support a blame culture in social work practice, and individual scapegoating when tragedies occur. We want to explore the concept, suggested by Webb (2001), that social work practice does indeed refer to evidence but cannot be wholly determined by a traditionally tried-and-tested theory which can be applied outside the understanding of individual agency, resilience and the local context.

What we are not trying to do in this chapter is to give you a re-run of all the literature written about evidence-based practice, and we would suggest that Webb (2006) will give you a thorough overview of the key issues and debates in this area. What we want to do is to ask you to extend your thinking around evidence-based practice beyond the traditional forms of exploration and start to consider the evidence that informs *your* practice. We want you to ask yourself how you are going to incorporate your academic learning into your day-to-day practice with service users and carers.

We think that this chapter may pose more questions than answers, so let's start the list with two pertinent areas for you to consider. The questions we discuss below are big ones. However, we really are trying to avoid an indulgent existential exploration. Equally, we do not want to arrogantly assume that we have definitive answers, but we do think that the consideration of evidence-based practice in social work needs first to establish how it is relevant to social workers in their day-to-day work.

Has evidence informed your own practice?

List the evidence that you have used in your own practice, study or both. Think about the main source of theory and knowledge that has been useful to you in either your practice or academic studies. What evidence has informed your practice?

ACTIVITY

Think about... Other voices to be heard about evidence-based practice

Are you confident that you could explain to a service user or carer the evidence that you are drawing on to inform your work with them?

What Evidence Do Social Workers Need to Do Their Job?

We suggest that social workers do many things, but that a large part of a frontline social worker's role is to undertake risk assessments and make decisions that arise from the evidence gathered by the social worker. In this section, we want to explore the evidence that social workers need in order to undertake accurate and safe assessments.

First, the large part of mainstream modern-day social work takes place within the climate of the assessment of risk and attention is paid to protection rather than in the delivery of therapeutic interventions. We are not suggesting that evidence-informed interventions do not have an important part to play in social work, but looking at the day-to-day practice of frontline social workers who have the job of working to protect people at risk, either children or adults, will highlight that the emphasis is very much on the assessment of risk and the analysis of it to ensure that vulnerable people are safeguarded wherever possible.

The historical debates on evidence-based practice have largely concentrated on the interventional aspects from a positivist perspective. Positivism has been defined as:

> The epistemological doctrine that physical and social reality are independent of those who observe them, and that observations of these realities, if unbiased, constitute scientific knowledge. (Webb, 2006: 18)

It may also be relevant to think about how these historical debates have often been referred to as 'evidence-based practice' rather than as 'evidence-based practice in *social work*', as Webb (2006) also points out. The discussion on positivism may lead you to think about the complexities of evidence-based practice in social work and to ask the question 'How does objectiveness fit with reflection in practice and where is experience of both the individual social worker and their managers in this equation?'

We highlighted in Chapter 1 how the whole area of evidence-based practice is both complex and challenging. The way in which social work as a profession is publically and politically examined when tragedies occur both determines the accountability of social work practice and also drives the way in which social workers are expected to practise (Higham, 2006). This in turn impacts on the choice of the knowledge base that is highlighted, often through procedure guidance (which often quickly dictates procedure) and is held as a panacea that claims it will reduce the likelihood of future tragedies. We want you to think about how the evidence from a validated knowledge base will inform your literature review and how this in turn will inform your own understanding of the literature and debates in social work evidence-based practice. We would also ask you to consider where this validated knowledge base has come from and how it connects, or not, to current social work practice.

In order to consider these areas, we need to explore the concept of validated knowledge that informs social work practice.

In identifying this knowledge base, it is useful to return to some of the discussion in Chapter 1, where we explored the concept of 'grey literature' and looked at how this informs the knowledge base for social workers in practice. We have looked at the importance of how policy documents impact upon social work practice and are instructive in directing the social worker to a specific area of knowledge. The knowledge that informs policy may not always be peer-reviewed, but it has a strong influence in public perception and policy development and this in turn feeds into the common-sense approach to social work which portrays social work as a task that anyone can do. As such, it reduces the positioning of social work activity as a professionally skilled job. Webb (2006) challenges the appropriateness of simplistic responses to risk in the form of low key reviews and technologies of care that are commonly used in social work practice settings.

In looking at the complexities of the knowledge base that informs evidence-based social work practice, it is appropriate to consider the strength of the influence of the public and political views that can dominate and assume expertise in how social work should be delivered and, in doing this, decide on the knowledge that should inform the evidence base for practice. For example, think about how the furore of disapproval swept through the media and government in November 2012 when three children in a UK Children's Services Department were allegedly removed from foster carers because the carers were members of the UK Independence Party (UKIP). The media reported that the foster carers were deemed to be unable to meet the ethnicity needs of the children because of their political views in respect of immigration, identity and race. It transpired that the children were placed with these foster carers as a temporary measure until permanent foster carers could be found and, indeed, that the plan had always been for the children to move to another permanent placement. Now you may be thinking what has this got to do with evidence-based practice – well, bear with us! The knowledge base that informed the plan for these young children may have been located in the evidence that exists around attachment theory and the importance of securing a permanent attachment figure for children as soon as possible in their lives. Social work has a strong understanding of attachment issues and could have showcased this intention as the reason for the removal of the children. The response from the head of service was to fuel the media fire by referring only to the political views of the carers rather than establishing the strong evidence base from attachment theory that had informed the decision to remove the children. The response from the leader of the council to the public and politicians was the promise of an enquiry to look at why the children had been moved. This lack of visible confidence in the decisions made by social workers feeds into the 'common-sense' agenda that social work can be done by anyone with a sensible head on their shoulders. Perhaps this was really a missed opportunity to demonstrate the use of validated knowledge in decision making in social work practice, that is evidence-based practice in social work?

Risk Assessment and Evidence-based Practice

The use of knowledge as an evidence base to inform the assessment of risk has deep significance on many levels. First, the accuracy of the assessment of risk will seriously protect, or not, the person deemed to be at risk. This accuracy will be informed by the individual knowledge and skills of the social worker as well as the efficacy of the supervision structure for the social worker, the legal requirements of the assessment, the individual capacity and strengths of the service user and, very importantly, the resource allocated to the risk assessment task. The context in which the assessment takes place (i.e. the agency and the policies of the agency) and the wider influences of legal requirements will determine both timescales and the nature of the theory to be used as the evidence on which to base judgements in these assessments of risk.

You need to consider social work theory in its widest context (e.g. communication, observation, emotional understanding and literacy) and, more specifically, in relation to the detailed knowledge around child development, illness, psychological and physical understandings, the way that stress and distress impact upon behaviour, defence mechanisms, loss and bereavement, and risk assessment.

How Do Social Workers Use the Evidence to Support Their Assessment of Risk?

Whether you are working with adults or children, you will be required to produce reports of your assessments that are rigorously supported with evidence to justify your recommended course of action. Social workers engage with assessment of risk in a broad spectrum of practice areas, such as in criminal justice, community care, child protection and mental health settings.

ACTIVITY

Where is the evidence to support your decision?

You have been asked to produce a report for a Mental Health Review Tribunal. You will need to demonstrate that you have considered the risk factors in relation to the decisions made regarding this particular service user.

Karen is 25 years old and has recently given birth to a baby girl. Her partner contacted the GP as Karen had made a threat to end her own life. The GP called on the psychiatrist and you, as the Approved Mental Health Professional (AMHP), supported an application for Karen to be admitted for assessment. Karen has a history of depression and trauma following her childhood experiences of sexual abuse.

What are your immediate thoughts about risks for Karen and her family?

As the AMHP, you have explored community provision but concluded with medics that the only safe place for Karen at this point in time is to be admitted for assessment. Has the evidence to support your judgement been informed by specific knowledge about the risks faced by someone in Karen's position? Can you identify how your own practice experience supports the evidence that you have drawn upon to inform your judgement if you were working as an AMHP on the above case?

ACTIVITY

Alicia

You are a postgraduate student supported by your employer to complete an MA in Child Protection. Your employer has asked you to focus your literature review on the knowledge that will inform evidence-based practice in the case of the following young woman:

Alicia is 15 years old and has recently been placed on a care order as her parents have refused to let her live in the family home. They say that Alicia has been out of control for a long time and they have tried their best. They have told the social worker that Alicia has recently started to take her younger sister Petra, who is 12 years old, with her when she goes out to meet older men. The parents say that Petra has already arrived home with new clothes and jewellery that she could not have afforded to buy for herself. They also describe Petra as being tearful and moody and reluctant to go to school or meet with any of her friends.

Now draw up a list of some of the knowledge that will inform an evidence-based approach to the situation for Alicia and her family.

Decision making

When did you last make a decision?

It may have been to have coffee rather than tea or to eat a sandwich at your desk instead of going to the gym? Whatever the decision, try to list the factors that influenced your decision and impacted on you.

It may be that available information played a part in this decision making, or was it just a whim? Either way, the way you approach personal decision making may impact upon your professional decisions.

What are the factors that inform the decision-making processes in social work?

- Information
- Resources
- Knowledge and skills
- Legal requirements
- Experience
- Reflection

Think about... What do social workers need to know?

At this point we would like to pose our earthshattering question of 'What knowledge do social workers need to do the job?'

- List some aspects of your own knowledge base for the theory that has informed your practice.
- Think about when this theory was developed and published.
- Do you need an update?

Another challenge to more traditional scientific approaches is the potential for social work to become a restricted activity that does not value individual judgement and understandings. The necessity to maintain the opportunity for social workers to make judgements based on specific knowledge is highlighted by the Reform Board recommendations in the identification of the importance of intuitive practice (Reform Board, 2010).

This is highlighted alongside the importance of social workers being trained and supported to develop their resilience to deal with the stress of the job and the scrutiny that has become a significant factor in the day-to-day practice of frontline workers. We are not suggesting that social workers should be exempt from this level of public surveillance, but we are proposing that the scapegoating culture that has been evident in agencies when tragedy has occurred is neither productive nor preventative in respect of developing social work practice. The preoccupation with knowledge that mainly addresses theoretical perspectives can lead to a denial of the importance of the role of both reflection and experience in social work practice.

As Webb (2006) affirms in his critique of evidence-based practice that is singly informed and demonstrates a lack of recognition of experience gained over time from working in social work settings with specific service users and carers, one of the problems of looking at a systematic approach to knowledge denies the opportunity to look at the exceptions to the rules. For example, how can we explain that two people with seemingly very similar experiences of the care system develop into very different adults? How can the different adults with different lives and degrees of success be understood and recognised in a knowledge validation process that looks at a majority and does not give attention to individual agency and the ability of individuals to contradict the expectations? This ability to defy the expectations cannot simply be explained by the 'exception that proves the rule'. It challenges the concept of a system of validated knowledge that does not include a consideration of why certain service users defy the norm by leading lives that totally challenge expectations that are based on the scientifically validated theory/knowledge. The relevance of the evidence base for social work practice discussion is one that is sometimes regarded by more cynical, experienced practitioners as being solely the domain of students who are studying on qualifying courses. Some experienced practitioners may lack confidence in putting forward a theoretical base to their practice and, indeed, may see the pursuit of theory by students as an activity that is somehow detached from real social work. The shift from therapeutic interventions to risk assessments and protection highlighted earlier in this discussion may in some way account for the apparent cynicism towards theory from busy and stressed frontline social workers. Indeed, the prescriptive procedural guidance on protection in children and family and adult work supports this position (Ferguson, 2011).

The problem of undervaluing the importance of evidence in social work decision making, along with discretion and reflection, has been highlighted by Munro (2011). In her work, she clearly calls for social workers to draw on evidence and, at the same time, develop intuition based on experience. Social workers should be confident in listening to the concerns raised before them and their organisations, developing supervision support to help social workers find ways of interpreting concerns in order to protect children.

It may also be that experienced social workers are working in organisations that they regard as being unsupportive in the application of theory to practice (Reform Board, 2010). The converse of this is the active support of theory from social workers working within a specific area that showcases a particular emphasis on the use of theory to support practice (e.g. specialist practitioner roles that have a specific theory requirement).

It is in this context that the debates around evidence-based practice are positioned and the development of your understanding of how evidence-based discussions have progressed will be useful in your own review of the literature that is specific to your area of study.

We may not have answered our over-ambitious question of 'What evidence do social workers need to do their job?', but perhaps we have planted the seed in your mind that the social work-specific task will influence the choice of evidence base it relies upon?

The specific nature of the social work task is highlighted in the discussion on the use of knowledge of child development in relation to outcomes for children. Brandon et al. (2008) looked at Serious Case Reviews (SRCs) in relation to the application of knowledge on child development and drew upon evidence of the negative impact of maltreatment on both the developmental progress and well-being of the child.

They categorised this in three age bands: in infancy they found that injury affected attachment and growth and caused developmental delay; in later childhood there was evidence of anxiety and mood disorders, disruptive behaviour, academic failure and poor peer relations; in adolescence the likely effects included conduct disorder, alcohol abuse, other risk-taking behaviours and recurrent victimisation (http://dera. ioe.ac.uk/7190/1/dcsf-rr023.pdf).

It is in this context of looking at the wide range of social work practice, and the evidence that supports it, that we are asking you to explore the literature that you consider as part of your literature review. The application to social work practice of the knowledge that you explore will facilitate your critique of the areas that you consider in your literature review. It is a bold assertion that all the knowledge that you will explore will have a relevance to social work practice, but it is one that we would like to propose. Indeed, we suggest that you look actively for the relevance and applicability as a matter of course.

You will already have assessed that the concepts surrounding evidence-based practice are complex and will need to be considered in relation to understandings that have been informed by the recent debates in both child and adult protection. We want to pose some further questions for you to consider in relation to evidence on which you practise:

- Historically, pure evidence-based practice was often associated with behaviourist approaches, so how does this restrictive view accommodate other theoretical approaches?
- How does evidence-based practice support decision making in social work and where is the place of individual and intuitive understanding in the making of these decisions?

Chapter Summary

- We have started the exploration of evidence-based practice for you to consider as you progress with your literature review.
- We have looked at why social workers use evidence to inform their practice.
- We have explored some of the published work in this field.
- We have raised questions for you about your own evidence-based practice.

Further Reading and Useful Resources

The following website will give you an introduction to some of the early discussions on evidence-based practice and consideration of how evidence from research can impact on resources in social work.

www.scie.org.uk/publications/reports/report10.pdf

Community Care Inform – The Online Resource for Professionals Working with Children and Families: www.ccinform.co.uk/

Community Care Inform is an online resource for childcare social workers that provides up-to-date research on key issues in childcare social work practice. It is supported by an editorial team from both practice and academic settings and is available by subscription via agency/educational establishments. The main aims of the resource are to enable childcare social workers to:

- evidence their social work practice
- stay up to date with research, legislation, case law and guidance
- build professional confidence
- improve outcomes for children and young people.

References

Brandon, M., Belderson, P., Warren, C., Howe, D., Gardener, R., Dodsworth, J. and Backs, J. (2008) *Analysing Child Deaths and Serious Injury through Abuse and Neglect: What Can We Learn?* Research Report DCSF-RR023. Available at: http://dera.ioe.ac.uk/7190/1/dcsf-rr023.pdf (accessed 12 December 2012).

Ferguson, H. (2011) *Child Protection Practice*. Basingstoke: Palgrave Macmillan.

Higham, P. (2006) *Social Work: Introducing Professional Practice*. London: Sage.

Munro, E. (2011) *The Munro Review of Child Protection: Final Report, a Child-centred System*. London: The Stationery Office (TSO).

Reform Board (2010) *Building a Safe and Confident Future*. Available at: www.hcp-uk.org/assets/documents/10003287Building-a-safe-and-confident-future-detailedproposals.pdf (accessed 12 December 2012).

Webb, S.A. (2001) 'Some considerations on the validity of evidence-based practice in social work', *The British Journal of Social Work*, 31(1): 57–79.

Webb, S.A. (2006) *Social Work in a Risk Society*. Basingstoke: Palgrave Macmillan.

Glossary of Terms and Abbreviations

Abstract   A brief summary of a journal article, report, dissertation or other type of research output or academic publication. It provides an overview of the question or issue the work is addressing, the research approach that has been used, a brief summary of the results and the main findings. Sometimes reports feature an 'Executive Summary' instead of an abstract, but this fulfils the same kind of role.

AMHP   Approved Mental Health Professional

ASSIA   Applied Social Sciences Index and Abstracts. This is an indexing and abstracting tool that covers areas including health, social services, psychology, sociology, economics, politics, race relations and education.

Boolean operators   These are linking words that can be used to broaden, narrow and refine your online and database searching. Search terms and keywords can be linked together using Boolean operator words such as 'AND', 'NOT' and 'OR'. It is always best to consult search facilities' 'help' sections to see if Boolean operators are supported.

Cochrane Reviews   These are systematic reviews of primary research that focus on human health care and health policy. They are seen as the 'gold standard' in systematic literature reviews.

Critical appraisal   As the term suggests, critical appraisal involves being critical (asking probing questions) in the pursuit of trying to appraise (weigh up or evaluate) the strength of evidence and argument presented within a piece of work.

Data extraction   Refers to the process of collecting relevant data from the mass of journal articles, reports, grey literature and other materials that make up your literature base. This process can be challenging as data may be inconsistently presented across a number of different publications. Effective data extraction allows for comparisons across different studies and for data synthesis (i.e. bringing data from different sources together).

Empirical research   Describes research that is designed to establish knowledge about things in the world through processes of direct and indirect observation. It is based on a philosophical view of the world that views evidence gained through sensory experience as the basis of knowledge and understanding.

EndNote   A commercial software package that allows users to save their own libraries of reference material, manage their references and easily generate citations and reference lists using plug-ins like 'Cite While You Write', which is designed to work with Microsoft Word.

Evidence-based practice   Refers to practice that is informed by available research evidence and/or published expertise based on evidence.

Evidence-informed approaches   These kinds of approaches advocate that empirical data and research evidence must be considered alongside other forms of knowledge and experience, including practitioner knowledge, user and carer knowledge, organisational knowledge, research knowledge and policy community knowledge.

Grey literature   Describes documents that have not been published through conventional routes. Grey literature includes newsletters, pamphlets, meeting minutes, internal reports, etc. It can be trickier to find and access 'grey literature'. Its name derives from the fact that it occupies a 'grey area' in comparison to traditional forms of published material.

Harvard referencing system   A popular referencing system used by many UK higher education institutions. It consists of a brief citation in the main body of the work that links, by author surname and year of publication, to a specific, full reference listed alphabetically at the end of the piece of work.

Keywords   In terms of research processes and, more specifically, literature searches, keywords are the primary search words or terms used to focus and target the search process. Keywords are usually identified from the research question, essay/assignment title or research brief. They should be relevant to the research topic and should help to weed out anything that is irrelevant. The set of keywords that a researcher uses will often develop and change throughout the literature search process.

Literature (or 'the literature')   A shorthand way of referring to the sum of published knowledge about a particular subject. This will take the form of books, academic journals, practitioner journals, reports, websites, data repositories and other sources.

Meta-analysis   A form of analysis applied across multiple studies in order that patterns, correspondences, inconsistencies, divergencies and other kinds of relationships can be identified and examined.

Methodology   Literally 'the study of methods', a methodology is the framework that guides the way research is carried out. The choice of methodology will usually suggest the most appropriate types of research method for data collection and what methods of data analysis are most useful.

Narrative literature reviews   A common type of literature review that is mainly concerned with drawing together conceptual and theoretical ideas from a range of literature. They are usually not as transparent in terms of process, or as comprehensive in terms of coverage, as systematic literature reviews.

Non-empirical studies Studies that do not draw on either empirical data or research that uses empirical data. Usually, then, non-empirical studies are not based on evidence drawn from the 'real-world', but often draw primarily on conceptual, theoretical or philosophical material and ideas.

Peer-review The process of scrutinising, appraising and evaluating a piece of work by a group of peers from a related discipline area. It is used widely in the field of academic research and publishing. The main purpose of the peer-review process is to maintain quality and standards in relation to academic work, including research.

Plagiarism The act of presenting someone else's work or ideas as if they are your own.

Primary research Primary research is where the researcher collects their own original (or primary) data, which they then later analyse in order to produce primary research findings.

Qualitative data Data that can take a wide number of forms, including word-based and image-based data. Research that uses qualitative data allows the researcher to explore people's thoughts, experiences, emotional states and other subjective aspects of experience. Examples of qualitative data include written interview transcripts and video documentation from direct observations.

Qualitative data synthesis (QDS) An approach to data synthesis that is concerned with identifying common themes across primary, qualitative research studies.

Quantitative data Data that can be measured or quantified in some way, and is therefore number-based. Research that uses quantitative data usually seeks to establish objective, measurable statements about the world. Examples of quantitative data include questionnaire data and transaction logs (e.g. how frequently a task is performed).

Reliability Broadly speaking, reliability is a measure of how stable and consistent a research method is, so that if the research were to be repeated in the same way at a later date, one could confidently expect to achieve similar results.

SCR Serious Case Reviews

Statistical meta-analysis The process of extracting data from a number of studies, and then combining it to allow reviewers to carry out statistical analysis on the combined data.

Systematic literature reviews A particular type of literature review that is rigorous, systematic and transparent in terms of how the review process is devised and carried out. Systematic reviews usually have a very well-defined focus, are guided by an explicit review protocol and aim for comprehensiveness in terms of coverage of the literature.

Systematic review protocols The frameworks developed to guide the process of carrying out specific systematic literature review processes to ensure consistency, accuracy and transparency.

Validity In very general terms, validity is a measure of how 'fit for purpose' a research method is. So, in considering validity, we might ask whether the research method actually measures what it has been used to measure and, if so, how effectively it does this. Ways of measuring validity differ for different types of research.

Zotero A free, open-source reference management program that allows users to create their own libraries of reference materials and has plug-ins to enable compatibility with word-processing software.

Index

Page numbers in *italics* refer to tables.